PATCHWORK GRANNY SQUARE BLANKETS

Learn to Crochet
Quilt-Inspired Throws,
Home Décor & More

ANITA GIBNEY

Quarto.com

First Published in 2025 by Quarry Books, an imprint of The Quarto Group,
100 Cummings Center, Suite 265-D, Beverly, MA 01915, USA.
T (978) 282-9590 F (978) 283-2742

EEA Representation, WTS Tax d.o.o.,
Žanova ulica 3, 4000 Kranj, Slovenia.
www.wts-tax.si

ISBN: 978-0-7603-9625-4

Digital edition published in 2025
eISBN: 978-0-7603-9626-1

Library of Congress Cataloging-in-Publication Data is available.

Design: Samantha J. Bednarek, samanthabednarek.com
Cover Image: Leanne Dixon
Page Layout: Samantha J. Bednarek, samanthabednarek.com
Stylist: Claire Montgomerie
Photographer: Leanne Dixon
Illustration: Anita Gibney

To Mark. My husband,
best friend, and
number-one person.

CONTENTS

67

CHAPTER 3

THE PROJECTS

INTRODUCTION

In the mid-1970s, a very small me discovered the *Golden Hands* series of craft magazines. At the time, I could barely read but was utterly captivated by the pictures—to be more specific, the yarn pictures. I would skip past all the sewing ones, looking for the next yarny delight. Knitting, crochet, tapestry, I loved them all. It was a combination of the bright colors and seeing the possibilities of a material that was so familiar to me.

My mum always had knitting on the go, so we spent a lot of time in yarn shops! Mum taught me to knit, and I was very adept at holey garter scarves. I would sit in rapt silence, tongue sticking out in concentration while squeaking my way through row after row. Now and then, probably when the squeaking became too unbearable, my mum would loosen off my stitches for me, and off I'd go again.

When my children were babies, I knitted all sorts of little garments and learned to read patterns and knit without holes (mainly). I have a picture of my son in the hat and mittens I made, looking thoroughly unimpressed and a little bit terrified.

As the years passed, I explored all kinds of different crafts, spending several years teaching design and technology. Nothing builds character quite like a room full of teenagers with woodworking tools! My dad always encouraged me to try anything practical, so I'm just as happy with a power tool as I am with a paintbrush. But I realized I was missing the special kind of comfort that only yarn can bring.

I eventually came full circle and rediscovered my love for yarn around 15 years ago. I picked up a hook one day and haven't put it down since. Barely a day goes by when I am not involved in some kind of yarn-related activity. If I'm not doing something with yarn, you can bet I'm thinking about it!

I am completely fascinated by granny squares, and they feature heavily in my designs. They are the humblest and most traditional crochet designs but infinitely and exquisitely versatile. This book is a tribute to the granny square and just one of the ways in which they can shine at the center of a design.

I hope the designs within inspire you and leave you with a little sense of my granny square joy.

HOW TO USE THIS BOOK

This book is divided into sections to guide you through the process of making patchwork granny square blankets and accessories. If you are very new to crochet, I suggest starting right at the beginning and reading through chapter 1 (p. 15), which covers the basic techniques. I detail the stitches used, joining techniques, and other helpful information. Chapter 2 (p. 39) gives instructions for making twelve different quilt blocks in crochet, and chapter 3 (p. 67) brings everything together in a selection of projects for your home.

MIXING AND MATCHING TECHNIQUES

Almost all the blocks and projects can be made using your choice of joining technique. I have shown my examples in the various methods described in the techniques section (p. 30), but it is entirely up to you which one you use for your own blocks. Confession time: I always avoid sewing crochet squares together if possible. Single crochet joins or the join-as-you-go (JAYG) method work better for me. However, if you enjoy sewing, go for it! Once you have tried a couple of the blocks, you will get a feel for what type of join you prefer.

YARN CHOICE

Your choice of yarn can drastically change the appearance of a piece. I've made the Lavender Path Baby Blanket (p. 69) in delicate 4 ply merino to make it suitable for a baby. The same design worked in a vibrant chunky yarn would be perfect for a teenager. Please don't feel restricted by my examples. Try experimenting with different color schemes and yarn weights to create your masterpieces. More information about choosing yarn is on page 12.

BLANKET SIZING

As well as changing the size of a blanket with your choice of yarn weight, you can change the size of most of the designs by adding more or fewer blocks. Visit the supplemental materials on page 140 for more information. I have tried to ensure that the border instructions for each design will work and do not need any modifications, even if you have used a different number of blocks.

CREATING YOUR OWN DESIGNS

I hope this book inspires you to experiment and create your own designs. Once you have mastered the basics, it's possible to recreate virtually any quilt design in crochet. To get you started, I've provided templates you can use to help you design your own blocks (p. 137). Trace or photocopy them and get to work with the colored pencils. It's fun to come up with new layouts.

Most importantly, enjoy the process and have fun!

TOOLS & MATERIALS

One of the joys of crochet is that you need only the absolute minimum of equipment to start enjoying this craft. If you're new to crochet, over the next few pages I share the essentials. Plus, I talk about some extras which are nice to have in your kit. These will last you for years to come! I also share helpful information on choosing yarns. For those with more experience, skip to chapter 1 (p. 15) to start learning about making the components that go into patchwork crochet blocks.

HOOKS

If you've picked up this book, I'm guessing you already know that crochet is worked with a hook. But did you know that there are different types of hooks, and that you might like one hook design more than another? It's a good idea to experiment with different types to find what type is most comfortable for you to use.

Basic aluminum or bamboo hooks are inexpensive, but depending on how you hold them, they may be uncomfortable to crochet with for long periods. You may find a more ergonomic hook with a molded grip is more comfortable. Try a few different hooks before committing to buying a large set.

The hook itself can be set one of two ways. Inline looks as if a notch was cut out of a straight line and the end is as wide as the shaft. Tapered has a head slightly smaller than the body of the hook. The hook design is another feature left to personal preference. However, some people find the hook with a tapered head easier to work into tight stitches.

Hooks are measured by the diameter of their shaft. In the United States, hooks are given alphabet labels with a few exceptions, while in the United Kingdom they're measured in millimeters (mm). The projects in this book use E/4 (3.5 mm), G/6 (4 mm), 7 (4.5 mm), and H/8 (5 mm) hooks. Changing your hook size will change the size of your stitches and the density of your fabric. If something feels too tight, try a bigger hook. If it is too loose, try a smaller hook.

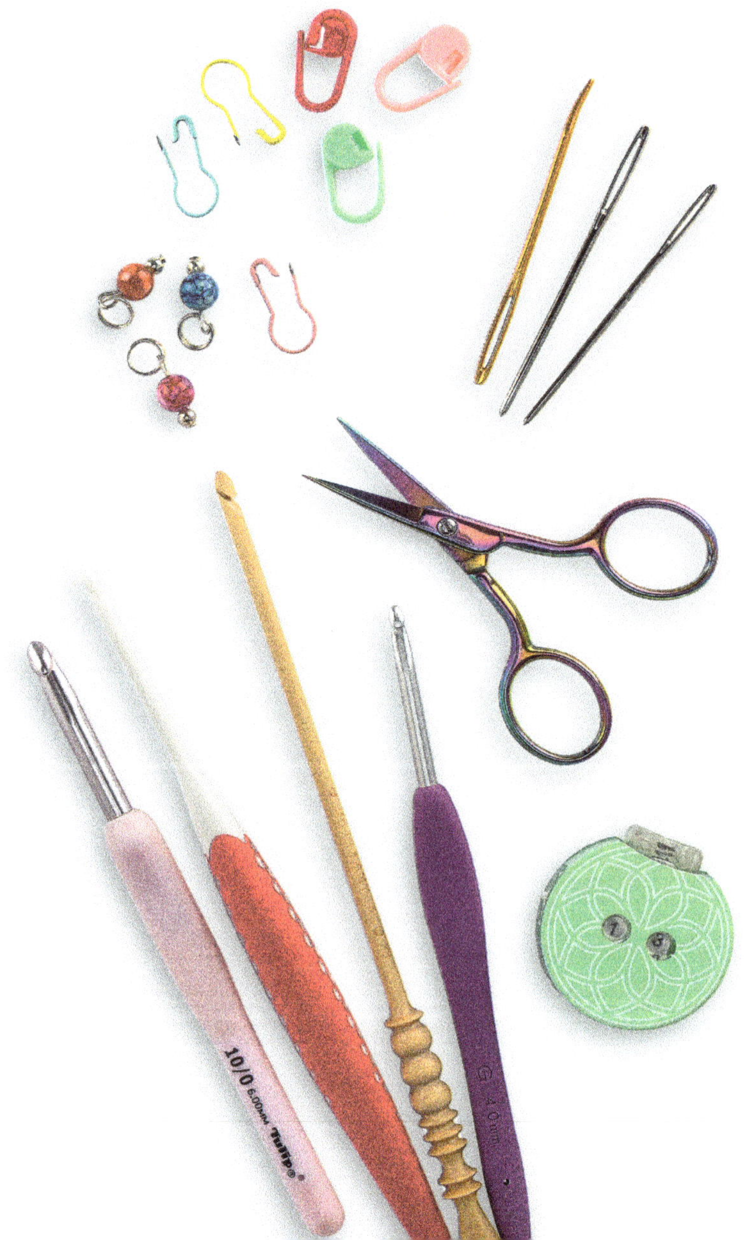

SCISSORS

You will need a small pair of sharp scissors to cut your yarn. Embroidery scissors or snips are ideal for this.

NEEDLES

Blunt-end yarn or tapestry needles are a must for weaving in ends and sewing pieces together. I have a couple with different-sized eyes for varying weights of yarn.

NOTEPAD AND PEN

No crochet bag should be without a notepad and pen! They allow you to make pattern notes (what row were you on), track yarn information (recording the dye lot of a color should you run out), and hooks used (maybe you used a size H/8 for the blocks and a G/6 for the edging). I can never remember all the details of a project, so it's reassuring to have them written down.

STITCH MARKERS

A handful of stitch markers are worth their weight in gold for crocheters. You can use them to mark the right side of your work (which is easy to lose track of with large and complex projects), help with stitch counts, or hold pieces together so they are in the right place for joining. They come in several different styles, but I find the locking ones that look like little safety pins are the most useful.

HELPFUL EXTRAS

MEASURING TAPE AND RULER

I keep a small steel rule in my kit bag to accurately measure small pieces. A tape measure is handy for larger pieces.

ROW COUNTER

If your pattern involves many rows, a row counter can help you keep track of where you are, particularly if you put your project down and return to it many hours later!

BLOCKING EQUIPMENT

A blocking board, foam mats and rust-free pins, and spray bottle or steamer are all useful for blocking but not essential. I've only recently acquired these items, managing to block perfectly well for many years with my ironing board and steam iron.

CASES AND PROJECT BAGS

A small bag to keep your hooks and bits and bobs in is handy to have. A pencil case is ideal for this. A project bag is useful for keeping your yarn and project together and clean, especially if you are on the move with it. I have a much loved and extremely battered basket that follows me around the house and on my travels. You will spot it in this book if you keep an eye out.

YARNS

Choosing the best yarn for your project can greatly affect the finished item's appearance and feel. The good news is that blankets and throws are very forgiving when it comes to yarn choice. Here are a few pointers to help you.

YARN WEIGHT

There are many different weights of yarn. But for the projects in this book, I've chosen four that are most suitable for making blankets and throws.

Fingering/4ply: This is a lightweight yarn suitable for delicate projects such as baby blankets. Because it's fine and worked with a small hook, it takes longer to work than thicker yarn.

Sport/DK: This is a real all-rounder and suitable for most blankets and throws. It's easier on the hands than some thicker yarns and is available in the largest variety of colors and textures.

Worsted/Aran: This is a versatile medium-weight yarn. It makes a warm fabric and is durable, making it ideal for blankets that will work hard!

Bulky/Chunky: Thicker yarns make snuggly blankets. They work up quickly and are a good choice if you need to make a quick gift.

The projects in this book are suitable for any weight yarn. The instructions for each block give you a guide to the finished size of each of the above yarns when worked with the recommended hook size.

FIBER

The fiber you choose depends on several factors, from texture and feel to ease of use. Acrylic is affordable, washable, and readily available. In a DK weight, acrylic is ideal for beginners as it is soft, strong, and forgiving if you need to unravel your work. Cotton yarn is cool and breathable, and also quite heavy. Wool and wool blend yarns are more expensive but have a beautiful and luxurious finish.

TIP Visit a local yarn store if you can. Seeing and feeling the yarns is good before deciding which is best for your project. They are also the best place to get expert help and advice.

COLOR

Color choice is very personal. Try to use colors you love and that inspire you. Nature is an excellent source of inspiration for this. Consider yarn textures and effects as well. Tweedy or yarns with nepps add visual interest, and variegated yarns can create striking effects when used in your patchwork blocks. Word to the wise, though, your stitches are easier to see when using lighter colors.

8/0 5.00MM Tulip®

CHAPTER 1

THE TECHNIQUES

One of the things I love most about crochet is its creative potential, and how simple stitches can be combined to create stunning effects. This chapter explores the techniques you'll need to transform your stitches into the building blocks of patchwork granny square designs.

You don't need to be an experienced crocheter to tackle these projects. I'll begin with the basics and guide you step by step, sharing tips and tricks to help you achieve beautiful results every time.

STITCHES AND TERMS

There are regional differences for crochet terms. This book uses U.S. terms, but I've provided the translations below if you are based in the U.K. or elsewhere. These are all the crochet terms you'll need for the projects in this book. I've included a brief overview of each stitch to walk you through them!

CHAIN (ch)

Make a slipknot and place it on your hook. Hold the end below the slipknot between your finger and thumb and pass the yarn from the ball over the hook. This is called "Yarn over." Pull the yarn through the loop on the hook to make a chain. Continue to yarn over and pull yarn through the loop until you have made the required number of chains.

Your hook should pass easily through the loop on your hook. If you find you have to tug to pull through, this means your chains are too tight. When you yarn over, try not to pull the yarn from the ball too tightly. You need just enough tension to keep it in place while pulling your hook through.

Counting Chains

You'll notice that each chain looks like a "V." When counting your chains, don't include the loop on your hook; just count the V shapes below it.

Chain

ABBREVIATIONS

U.S TERM		**U.K. TERM**	
Chain (s)	ch	Chain(s)	ch
Slip stitch	sl st	Slip stitch	sl st
Skip	sk	Skip	sk
Single crochet	sc	Double crochet	dc
Double crochet	dc	Treble crochet	tr
Double crochet two together	Dc2tog	Treble crochet two together	Tr2tog
Square brackets mean the instruction inside is repeated. The pattern will say how many times.	[ ]	Square brackets mean the instruction inside is repeated. The pattern will say how many times.	[ ]

Slip Stitch

Single Crochet

Half Double Crochet

SLIP STITCH (sl st)

In these projects, I have used the slip stitch to complete rounds by joining to the first stitch in the round, to move the yarn to a new position, and to join two separate pieces of crochet together.

To make a slip stitch, insert your hook into the indicated stitch or space. Unless the pattern says otherwise, this is usually from the front to the back of your work. Yarn over and pull the yarn through the stitch and the loop on your hook.

SINGLE CROCHET (sc)

(U.K. double crochet, dc)
Insert your hook into the indicated stitch or space. Yarn over and pull the yarn through the stitch. You will now have two loops on your hook. Yarn over and pull through both loops on your hook to complete the stitch.

HALF DOUBLE CROCHET (hdc)

(U.K. half treble crochet, htr)
Yarn over and insert your hook into the indicated stitch or space. Pull the yarn through the stitch. You will now have three loops on your hook. Yarn over and pull through all three loops on your hook to complete the stitch.

DOUBLE CROCHET (dc)

(U.K. treble crochet, tr)
Yarn over and insert your hook into the indicated stitch or space. Pull the yarn through the stitch. You will now have three loops on your hook. Yarn over and pull through two loops on your hook. You will now have two loops on your hook. Yarn over and pull through the remaining two loops to complete the stitch.

TIP Three double crochets worked into the same space or stitch are called a "double crochet cluster" or "granny cluster." You will see these frequently throughout this book!

Double Crochet

CROCHET BASICS

Once you've got the hang of basic stitches, it's time to expand your skills with a few basic techniques. Here, you'll learn how to join a new yarn when you've reached the end of a skein, how to change colors, how to fasten off a stitch, how to weave in ends (yes, you must do this), and more. These will become second nature very quickly as your skills grow.

JOINING YARN

You'll need to join a new yarn when joining individual squares to form a block or when joining blocks to make a blanket.

Fold over the yarn to form a loop, leaving a tail (also called an end) around 3" (7.5 cm) to weave in later. Pull the loop through the stitch or space where you want to join the yarn. Work a single crochet with both the yarn from the ball and the tail. This will create a neat and secure join that is easy to unpick if necessary. Drop the tail and continue working with the yarn from the ball only.

CHANGING COLORS

When making half-square triangle (p. 24) or quarter-square triangle (p. 26), you will need to change the color partway through a round. Color changes will always take place after a chain. To change to a new color, fold over the new color yarn to form a loop, leaving a tail of around 3" (7.5 cm) to weave in later. Pull the loop through the chain on your hook and continue working with the new color. The instructions for each square will tell you whether to crochet over the tail or not.

FASTENING OFF

Cut your yarn, leaving a tail around 3" (7.5 cm). Pull the tail through the final loop. You can do this with the loop on your hook or remove the hook and do it with your fingers. Pull tight so the loop closes against the edge of your work.

WEAVING IN ENDS

It's a good idea to weave in your yarn ends (or tails) as you go. It will not only save you a big task at the end of a project but also makes joining your individual squares into blocks much more manageable.

To weave in ends, begin on the wrong side of your work and thread the tail onto a yarn needle. Carefully insert the needle under a few nearby stitches, ensuring the yarn doesn't show on the right side. Don't pull too tightly, or you'll distort the shape. Catch the needle under a stitch again, hidden on the front, and weave it back in the opposite direction under several more stitches. Gently pull the yarn tail to secure it, then trim the excess yarn close to the woven-in end.

EDGING YOUR BLOCKS

Adding an additional round of stitches to your blocks not only gives a neat finish but can also make joining easier, or can provide a foundation for extra rounds to change the size or appearance of the block.

With the right side facing you, join your chosen yarn in any corner space and 1ch, 1sc, 2ch, 1sc in the same corner space to form a corner. Work 1sc in each stitch, including the corner spaces where squares meet. In each corner space work 1sc, 2ch, 1sc. When you have worked around all four sides of your block, sl st under both loops of the first sc to join. Fasten off and weave in ends.

Each individual granny square will have 11 stitches per side, 1 in each of the 9 stitches and 1 in each of the 2 corner spaces. This means that 3 square x 3 square blocks, such as Nine Patch, will have 33 stitches per side, and 4 square x 4 square blocks will have 44 stitches per side.

BLOCKING

Blocking your squares is not essential, but it enhances their appearance. Blocking will smooth out any unevenness, particularly in joins, help remove any curling, and improve the drape of your blanket. There are several techniques for blocking crochet, but all follow the same basic principles. I prefer to steam block my squares because it's quick. I also like to block the individual quilt blocks before joining them because smaller pieces are more manageable.

How to Block Your Squares

Begin by easing the block into the desired shape. You can do this on a wooden blocking board or using blocking mats and rust-free pins. Until recently, I had neither of these, so I blocked my squares by simply pinning them to the ironing board. Whichever you choose, try not to overstretch your block. The aim is to encourage it to be square and flat without distorting the stitches.

Now, apply some moisture. This can be a light misting of water from a spray bottle or steam from an iron or garment steamer. If using steam, ensure the iron or steamer doesn't touch the crochet. If your block is very distorted, you can soak it in warm water before pinning, but smaller pieces tend not to need this much attention.

Allow to dry/cool entirely before removing from the board or unpinning. This will allow the yarn to set into the new shape fully. This might take a few minutes if you are using steam or overnight if using water.

Store your blocks somewhere flat until you are ready to join them.

PATCHWORK COMPONENTS

In quilting, patchwork blocks are made from small "patches" of fabric. These patches are sewn together into bigger units that eventually become the finished block. Some of the units you may have heard of are half-square triangles and flying geese. To make crocheted patchwork blocks, we're going to use the mighty granny square to create our units and build our blocks! If you can make these components, you can make almost any traditional quilt block.

GRANNY SQUARES

The versatile granny square is the foundation of all the designs in this book. If you are familiar with granny squares, you may find my method slightly different from what you have done before. I make my squares without any chains between clusters on the sides and only two chains at the corners to give a neat, dense fabric. Turning your square over before commencing each round eliminates any twisting or skewing. This gives a better overall appearance when many squares are joined together.

1 **Round 1:** (Right Side) Make a slip knot, leaving a 3" (7.5 cm) tail, place it on your hook and 3ch. Sl st under both loops of the third chain from the hook to form a loop and 2ch. (The 2ch counts as the first dc.) 2dc into the loop. This forms your first granny cluster.

2 2ch, 3dc into loop. This forms your first corner.

3 2ch, 3dc into loop twice more. 2ch and sl st under both loops of the first dc (not the starting 2ch) to complete the round.

Note: By skipping the starting 2ch and slip stitching under both loops of the first dc, you will achieve a neat and virtually invisible join. This is important in single-color granny squares, particularly with lighter shades of yarn, as visible joins cause a prominent ridge.

1

2

3

4

5

4 **Round 2:** 2ch, turn.

2dc, 2ch, 3dc in the same corner space. [3dc, 2ch, 3dc in next corner space] 3 times. Sl st under both loops of the first dc to join.

5 **Round 3:** 2ch, turn. 2dc in the same space. [3dc, 2ch, 3dc in next corner space, 3dc in the next space] 3 times. 3dc, 2ch, 3dc in next corner space. Sl st under both loops of the first dc to join. Fasten off and weave in all ends.

HALF-SQUARE TRIANGLES

Half-Square Triangles (HSTs) are an essential building block of many quilt designs. They are made from two triangles of contrasting fabric sewn to form a square. Here, I will show you how to recreate them using crochet. This two-color square is based on the traditional granny square (p. 22). If you haven't done so already, I would recommend taking a look before starting the HSTs, as many of the stitches used are the same.

Color A – Blue   Color B – Cream

1 **Round 1:** (Right side) Using yarn A, 3ch, sl st in the third chain from the hook to form a loop and 3ch, (2dc, 2ch, 3dc) into the loop, working your stitches over the tail, 1ch.

Note: The 3ch at the start of the rounds counts as the first dc and one of the two granny square corner chains. You will sl st into the third chain to finish the round.

2 Join yarn B by pulling a loop through the 1ch. Work the rest of the round over the two ends (tails) to secure them.

3 Drop yarn A (do not carry it under your stitches). Using yarn B, 3dc, 2ch, 3dc into loop. 1ch, sl st in third chain of starting 3ch to join.

4 **Round 2:** 3ch, turn. 2dc in the corner space between yarn A and yarn B.

5 3dc, 2ch, 3dc in next corner space, 3dc in corner space between yarn B and yarn A. 1ch, drop yarn B and pick up yarn A by pulling a loop through the 1ch.

6 Complete the round in yarn A ending with a 1ch and sl st to join in third ch of starting 3ch.

7 **Round 3:** 3ch, turn. 2dc in corner space between yarn B and yarn A. 3dc in next space, 3dc, 1ch in next corner space. 3dc in next space, 3dc, 1ch, pick up yarn B. You can cut yarn A now, leaving a end to weave in later.

3dc in same space to complete corner. 3dc in next space, 3dc, 2ch, 3dc in corner space, 3dc in next space. 3dc in the corner space between yarn A and yarn B. 1ch, ss under both loops of third starting chain to join. Fasten off and weave in all ends.

1

2

3

4

5

6

7

QUARTER-SQUARE TRIANGLES

As the name suggests, quarter-square triangles (QSTs) are made from four right-angled triangles joined to form a square. In this crochet version, we will use the same technique as the HSTs but with additional color changes. Don't be afraid of working with multiple yarns at the same time. Practice with some scrap yarn and follow along step by step. QSTs are really just granny squares with color changes. It's quite intuitive when you get the hang of it.

If you are using the same color yarn more than once in your QST, you will need to use separate balls or wind a small amount off first.

Color A – Blue   Color B – Cream

Color C – Blue   Color D – Cream

1 **Round 1:** Using yarn A, make a slip knot, leaving a 3" (7.5 cm) tail. Place it on your hook and 3ch. Sl st under both loops of the third chain to form a loop and 3ch. 2dc, 2ch, 3dc into loop. 1ch.

Note: The 3ch at the start of each round counts as the first dc and one of the two granny square corner chains. You will sl st under both loops of the third chain to finish the round.

2 Join yarn B by pulling a loop through the 1ch. Work the rest of the round over the tails to secure them.

3 Drop yarn A (do not carry it under your stitches). Using yarn B, 3dc into loop. 1ch. Join yarn C by pulling a loop through the 1ch. Drop yarn B. Using yarn C, 3dc into loop. 1ch. Join yarn D by pulling a loop through the 1ch. Drop yarn C. Using yarn D, 3dc into loop. 1ch, sl st under both loops of the third chain of starting 3ch to join.

4 **Round 2:** 3ch, turn. 2dc in the corner space between yarn A and yarn D. Using yarn D, 3dc, 1ch in corner space. Pick up yarn C by pulling a loop through the 1ch. Drop yarn D (do not carry it under your stitches). Using yarn C, 3dc, 1ch in corner space. Pick up yarn B by pulling a loop through the 1ch. Drop yarn C. Using yarn B, 3dc, 1ch in corner space. Pick up

yarn A by pulling a loop through the 1ch. Drop yarn B. Using yarn A, 3dc, 1ch in corner space. Sl st under both loops of the third chain of starting 3ch to join.

3ch, turn. 2dc in the corner space between yarn A and yarn D. Using yarn A, 3dc in the next space, 3dc, 1ch in corner space. Pick up yarn B by pulling a loop through the 1ch. Drop yarn A (do not carry it under your stitches). Using yarn B, 3dc in the next space, 3dc, 1ch in the corner space. Pick up yarn C by pulling a loop through the 1ch. Drop yarn B. Using yarn C, 3dc in the next space, 3dc, 1ch in corner space. Pick up yarn D by pulling a loop through the 1ch. Drop yarn C. Using yarn D, 3dc in the next space, 3dc, 1ch in corner space. Sl st under both loops of the third chain of starting 3ch to join.

Fasten off and weave in all ends.

FLYING GEESE

Flying Geese quilt blocks are classic and versatile, adding movement to a design. While often used to represent birds in flight, they also lend themselves to abstract patterns. They are rectangular blocks twice as wide as tall, consisting of a larger "goose" triangle in the center flanked by two smaller "sky" triangles.

Color A – Green   Color B – Cream

In our crochet version, we will join two half-square triangles (HSTs, p. 24) using a technique called join-as-you-go (JAYG). This will turn the HSTs into a single unit, which can then be joined to other HSTs or squares to form a variety of different designs.

1 Start by making an HST (p. 24). Use yarn A as the color you want to be in the **center** or "goose" part of your flying geese block. In this example, I have used green as yarn A and cream as yarn B.

2 Make a second HST up to the end of Round 2. Begin Round 3 in the usual way with 3ch, turn. 2dc in corner space between yarn B and yarn A. 3dc in next space, 3dc, 1ch in next corner space. Instead of continuing the round, we will bring in the first HST and join the two together. You may find it helpful to do this on a flat surface, such as a table, until you get the hang of it.

Insert your hook from front to back into the 2ch space in the corner of your first HST.

Yarn over and sl st to join the two squares together.

Note: Always begin making your second HST with yarn A. This is the color you will join with, and you need to start with it to ensure you are in the right place when it is time to join using JAYG (p. 34).

1

2

3

4

5

3 3dc in the corner space to complete the corner of the second HST. Sl st in the next space on the side of the first HST. Once again, you are creating a join between the two squares. 3dc in the next space on the second HST.

4 Sl st in the next space on the side of the first HST and 3dc in the next space on the second HST.

5 Sl st in the next space on the side of the first HST and 3dc in the corner space on the second HST. Sl st into the corner space of the first HST and change to yarn B by pulling a loop through the sl st. You can cut yarn A now, leaving a tail to weave in later.

Complete Round 3 as you would a regular granny square. Fasten off and weave in all ends.

JOINING TECHNIQUES

There are a variety of ways to join your crocheted quilt block units with different positive and negative benefits. I encourage you to try all the techniques I explain here with a few of your practice granny squares to see which method suits your project best and gives you the look you are aiming for. I prefer to crochet my squares together and avoid sewing whenever I can.

WHIP STITCH JOIN

Whip stitch is a simple way to join two pieces of crochet together by sewing. It creates a flat, visible seam with a decorative appearance. This is great for giving the effect of a hand-sewn quilt.

You will need a yarn needle and a strand of yarn 1½ to 2 times the length of the seam you are sewing. This will ensure you have enough to complete the seam with one piece of yarn and a tail at each end to weave. If you want to highlight the stitching effect, you can use coordinating or contrasting yarn.

Place your squares together with the right sides facing. Join the yarn through the corner spaces of both pieces. You can fasten in place with a couple of stitches, but I prefer to use a single knot as it gives a neater finish.

Ensure your stitches are lined up and pass the needle through all loops of the corresponding pairs of stitches. Continue along the side of your square. Try not to pull the stitches too tight, as this will cause your seam to pucker.

SLIP STITCH JOIN

The slip stitch join is made using your crochet hook to work slip stitches through loops on two separate pieces of crochet to join them together. It's a simple technique that creates a less bulky seam than some other joining methods.

Place your squares together with the right sides facing. Place a slip knot on your hook and join the yarn through the corner spaces of both pieces.

Insert your hook through all loops of the next pair of corresponding stitches and yarn over. Pull the yarn through both pieces of crochet and then through the loop on your hook. Repeat along the edge of your square in each pair of stitches and finally in the last pair or corner spaces.

SINGLE CROCHET JOIN

The single crochet join is a sturdy and visible seam, often used when you want a strong, defined joint between crochet pieces. It's more substantial than the slip stitch join and can add a nice decorative touch. It's one of my favorite ways to join, as it looks as good on the back as it does on the front. For added interest and to frame your blocks, you can also use this join on the front of your work!

Place your squares together, right sides facing. Join your yarn through both corner spaces with a sc, using both the yarn from the ball and the tail.

Insert your hook through all loops of the next pair of corresponding stitches and yarn over.

Pull the yarn through both pieces of crochet. You will now have two loops on your hook.

Yarn over again and pull through both loops on your hook to complete the stitch.

Repeat along the edge of your square in each pair of stitches and finally in the last pair or corner spaces.

You can make your sc join through the back loops only as a variation and for an interesting, raised framing effect. The back loops are the two outermost loops of each square when the stitches are placed right sides together. Leaving the inner two loops disconnected creates a line of stitches around your block. You can see this in the Love Notes Throw (p. 117).

Joining Multiple Pairs of Squares

If you want to join more than one pair of squares, you do not need to fasten off between pairs. Instead, bring in the next pair of squares and continue in a single seam. This is the equivalent of chain piecing in quilting and will work with any of the joining techniques here.

JOIN-AS-YOU-GO (JAYG)

I will always use join-as-you-go if I can; it's my favorite way to join. It creates a clean, flat seam and eliminates the need for a separate joining step by joining the squares in the final round.

We've already seen the JAYG technique for making the flying geese unit (p. 28). This technique can be extended to all joins in most of the crochet blocks in this book.

JAYG Basics

When using JAYG, you are joining the granny squares, HSTs, or QSTs to each other during the last round. This means you don't have the additional step of joining them afterward.

Replace the corner chain or chains with slip stitches to join to the adjacent square or squares.

Slip stitch between 3dc clusters on the sides of your square to join it to the previous square or squares.

In the block instructions, if it's possible to do so, you will see instructions for what order to join your squares in if you want to use JAYG. It may be a little different than other joining methods.

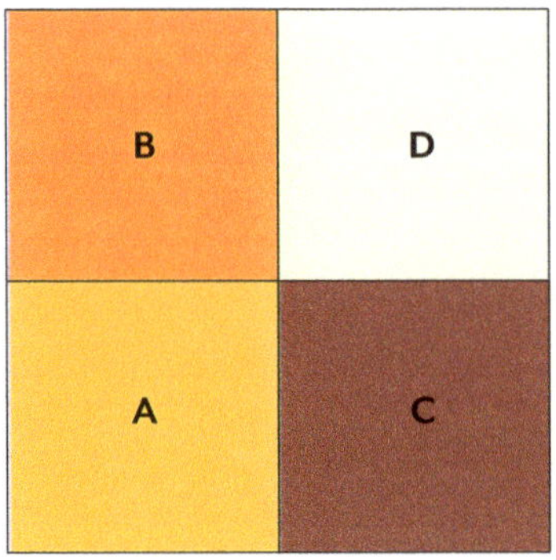

To Join Granny Squares

In this example, we'll use JAYG to connect squares B and C to square A. Note that this same technique used for the flying geese units.

1. Start by making a complete granny square (p. 22) (Square A). This is the bottom left corner. If you are left-handed, this can be the bottom right corner.

2. Make Square B up to the end of Round 2. Begin Round 3 in the usual way with 2ch, turn. 2dc in the same center space. 3dc in the corner space and 1ch. This is the first of the two corner chains. Instead of continuing the round, we will bring in Square A and join the two together.

   Insert your hook from front to back into the 2ch space in the corner of Square A.

   Yarn over and sl st to join the two squares together.

3 3dc in the corner space to complete the corner of the Square B. Sl st in the next space on the side of Square A. Once again, you are creating a join between the two squares. 3dc in the next space on Square B.

4 Sl st in the next space on the side of Square A and 3dc in the corner space of Square B.

5 Sl st in the corner space of Square A. This replaces the first corner chain and completes the join between the two squares. 1ch and complete the rest of the square as you would a regular granny square. You now have your bottom left square (A) with a square (B) joined above it.

6 Repeat steps 2–6 to join Square C to the right of Square A.

7 Now, join Square D on two sides in the space between Squares B and C. Make Square D up to the end of Round 2. Begin Round 3 in the usual way with 2ch, turn. 2dc in the same center. 3dc in the corner space and 1ch. Now, sl st into the corner space of Square B.

8 3dc in the corner space to complete the corner of Square D. Sl st in the next space on the side of Square B. 3dc in the next space on Square D.

9 Sl st in the next space on the side of square B and 3dc in the corner space of square D.

10 Sl st in the corner space of square B. This replaces the first corner chain. Now sl st in the corner space of square C. This replaces the second corner chain and completes the corner join.

11 3dc in the corner space to complete the corner of square D. Sl st in the next space on the side of Square C. 3dc in the next space on square D. Sl st in the next space on the side of Square C and 3dc in the corner space of square D. Sl st in the corner space of Square C. 1ch and complete the rest of the square as you would a regular granny square.

Joining HSTs and QSTs

The technique for joining HSTs and QSTs is the same as for joining granny squares.

For HSTs, always begin making your square (yarn A) with the color you want to join with. If you need to join your HST on two sides that are different colors, yarn A should be the color you want to join with first.

QSTs are quite fiddly to join using JAYG because of the multiple color changes. Although possible to do, I would choose another joining method for these. If you want to use JAYG, begin making your QST with the color you want to join with first (yarn A). Your second side join will be in yarn D.

CROCHET SASHING

In quilting, sashing refers to the strips of fabric sewn between quilt blocks. It's like the framework that separates and highlights each block in a quilt design. In this book, I have used various crochet techniques to replicate the effect of sashing.

Fireside Blanket, page 111

Love Notes Throw, page 117

Modern Medallion Blanket, page 123

Use sashing to visually separate the blocks and unify the design with a consistent, repeated element throughout the design. You can see this in the Fireside Blanket (p. 111). I have used bands of mixed double and granny clusters to separate the Ohio Stars and Flying Geese but bring the design together with bands of color. This visual separation allows each block to stand out and prevents the overall design from feeling cluttered.

Use sashing to add size and create separation between blocks so they stand out. In the Love Notes Throw (p. 117), I used additional rounds of double crochet to make space between the blocks. This throw also features a deep band of moss stitch, which gives the effect of a sashing border.

Use sashing as a design element in itself. In the Modern Medallion Blanket (p. 123), the bands of granny clusters worked back and forth in rows along the edges of the flying geese to form part of the design, giving structure by forming a frame around the other blocks.

To achieve granny rows that lay flat, it's necessary to use a special stitch called the double crochet two together (dc2tog) when working directly along the edge of joined granny squares. It's a decrease stitch that is made across the two corner spaces where granny squares meet. If you were to make a granny cluster in each corner space where squares meet, you would have too many stitches and your row would begin to ruffle. This decrease reduces the number of stitches, preventing the edge from becoming too wavy or stretched out. It's also used when adding a granny cluster border around a blanket of joined squares. It's only needed for the first row if working back and forth or the first round of a border.

Here's how to do it:

1 Make the first dc of your granny cluster in the right-hand corner space.

2 **Double Crochet 2 Stitches Together (dc2tog)**
Yarn over, insert your hook into the right-hand corner space, yarn over, and pull through (3 loops on your hook).

Yarn over, pull through 2 loops (2 loops on your hook).

Yarn over, insert your hook into the left-hand corner space, yarn over, and pull through (4 loops on your hook).

Yarn over, pull through 2 loops (3 loops on your hook).

Yarn over, pull through all 3 loops.

3 Make 1dc in the left-hand corner space to complete the granny cluster.

If you are left-handed, begin in the left-hand corner space and complete the stitch in the right-hand corner space.

If you look closely at the stitch, it looks like four stitches when viewed from the front, but because of the decrease, only has three stitches when viewed from above.

8/0

CHAPTER 2

THE BLOCKS

With the basic and essential techniques for making crochet units covered, it's time to combine them to create patchwork blocks. I've selected 12 of the most-loved traditional quilt designs to recreate in crochet. With the techniques from chapter 1, you will also be able to create many other quilt block designs. Grab some yarn and a hook, and don't be afraid to experiment!

Nine Patch, page 42

Sails, page 44

Chevrons, page 50

Bear Paw, page 52

Sawtooth Star, page 58

Ohio Star, page 60

Mother's Favorite, page 46

Dutchman's Puzzle, page 48

Log Cabin, page 54

Heart, page 56

Broken Dishes, page 62

Double Trailing Star, page 64

NINE PATCH

The Nine Patch block is one of the oldest quilt blocks. It was often the first block that young children were taught to make, as cutting and sewing is easy. Fabric waste is minimal, so they were popular for using scraps as well. Traditionally, a nine-patch quilt block comprises four squares in lighter fabrics and five contrasting darker squares, but you can use any colors you like.

YARN

Shown in: King Cole Merino Blend DK (100% wool: 114 yd [104 m]/1.75 oz [50 g]) and King Cole Majestic DK (50% wool, 30% acrylic, 20% polyamide: 132 yd [121 m]/1.75 oz [50 g]).

Color A – Pale Blue

Color B – Silver

Color C – French Navy

Color D – Petrol

Color E – Slate Blue

Color F – White

MAKE

- Four 3-round Granny Squares (p. 22) in background color F.
- Five 3-round Granny Squares, one each in contrast colors A–E.

Note that these blocks are a great way to use oddments and scraps of yarn. Make one 3-round granny square and weigh it. Then you can weigh your yarn scraps to see if there is enough to make the required number of squares.

FINISHED BLOCK DIMENSIONS

YARN WEIGHT	HOOK SIZE	APPROX. BLOCK SIZE
Sport/4ply	E/4 (3.5 mm)	6½" (16 cm)
Light Worsted/DK	G/6 (4 mm)	7½" (19 cm)
Worsted/Aran	H/8 (5 mm)	9" (23 cm)
Bulky/Chunky	J/10 (6 mm)	11" (28 cm)

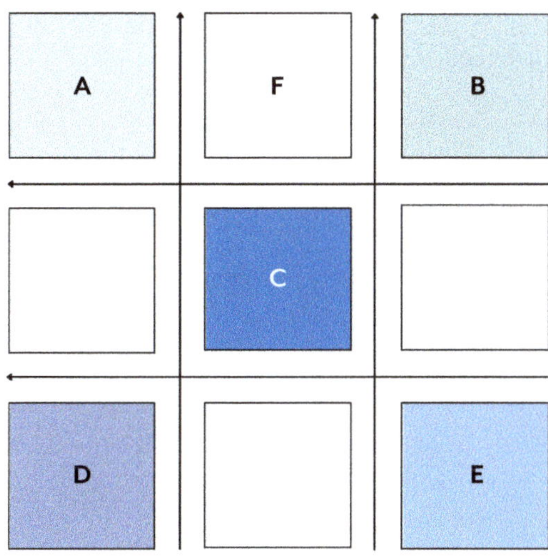

Fig. 1 Seamed

6	8	9
3	4	7
1	2	5

Fig. 2 JAYG

ASSEMBLE

Join the granny squares using your chosen joining technique (pp. 30–35). Make two continuous vertical joins first, followed by two horizontal joins (Fig. 1).

If using the JAYG method, start with the bottom left corner square and join in the order shown in the diagram (Fig. 2).

Weave in all ends.

OPTIONAL EDGING ROUND

Adding an edging round to your blocks is optional but, depending on the project, you may find it gives a neater finish and makes it easier to join the finished blocks. A round of single crochet can also form the foundation for further rounds to give the effect of sashing.

With the right side facing you, join your chosen yarn in any corner space. 1ch (does not count as a stitch), (1sc, 2ch, 1sc) in the same space to form a corner. 1sc in each stitch around including 1sc in each corner space where blocks join. Make (1sc, 2ch, 1sc) in the three remaining corner spaces, sl st into the first sc to join. Each side will have 33 sc, including corners. Block if required.

SAILS

I have called this block Sails because it reminds me of little sailing boats on the water. It is one of infinite combinations that can be made with the versatile HST. Before joining your individual HSTs, try rearranging them to see how many different designs you can create. It's really like magic!

YARN

Shown in: King Cole Majestic DK (50% wool, 30% acrylic, 20% polyamide: 132 yd [121 m]/1.75 oz [50 g]).

- Color A – White
- Color B – Duck Egg
- Color C – Grey
- Color D – Cloud
- Color E – Pale Petrol
- Color F – Sky Blue

MAKE

- Three Half-Square Triangles (HSTs, p. 24) using A and B.
- Three HSTs using A and C.
- Two HSTs using A and D.
- Four HSTs using A and E.
- Four HSTs using A and F.

FINISHED BLOCK DIMENSIONS

YARN WEIGHT	HOOK SIZE	APPROX. BLOCK SIZE
Sport/4ply	E/4 (3.5 mm)	8¼" (21 cm)
Light Worsted/DK	G/6 (4 mm)	10" (25 cm)
Worsted/Aran	H/8 (5 mm)	12" (30 cm)
Bulky/Chunky	J/10 (6 mm)	14½" (37 cm)

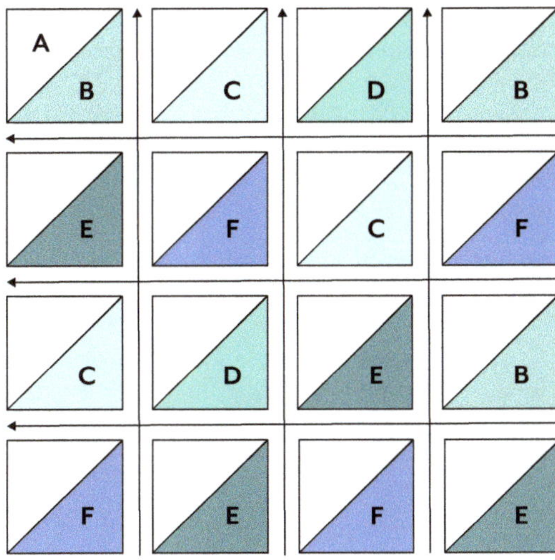

Fig. 1 Seamed

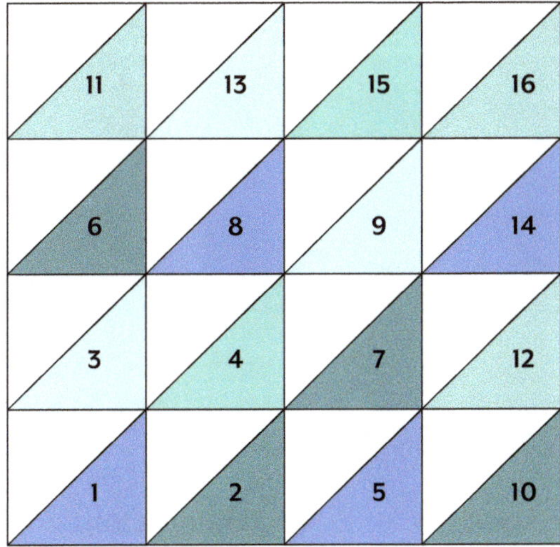

Fig. 2 JAYG

ASSEMBLE

Arrange the HSTs, following the diagram. Using your preferred joining technique (pp. 30–35), join the squares together, making the vertical seams first and then the horizontal seams (Fig. 1).

For the example shown, I used a single crochet join in the back loops only. Joining in the back loops only gives a decorative ridge, framing each square.

If using JAYG, start with the bottom left corner square and join in the order shown in the diagram. Be sure to begin making each HST with color A so you are in the correct place when it's time to join (Fig. 2).

Weave in ends.

OPTIONAL EDGING ROUND

With the right side facing you, join your chosen yarn in any corner space. 1ch (does not count as a stitch), (1sc, 2ch, 1sc) in the same space to form a corner. 1sc in each stitch around including 1sc in each corner space where blocks join. Make (1sc, 2ch, 1sc) in the three remaining corner spaces, sl st into the first sc to join. Each side will have 44 sc, including corners. Block if required.

MOTHER'S FAVORITE

The Mother's Favorite quilt block is striking as a standalone piece, but it truly shines when repeated multiple times. When combined with other blocks, it can create beautifully intricate patterns.

YARN

Shown in: King Cole Merino Blend DK (100% wool: 114 yd [104 m]/1.75 oz [50 g]).

- Color A – White
- Color B – Turquoise
- Color C – Thyme
- Color D – Sage

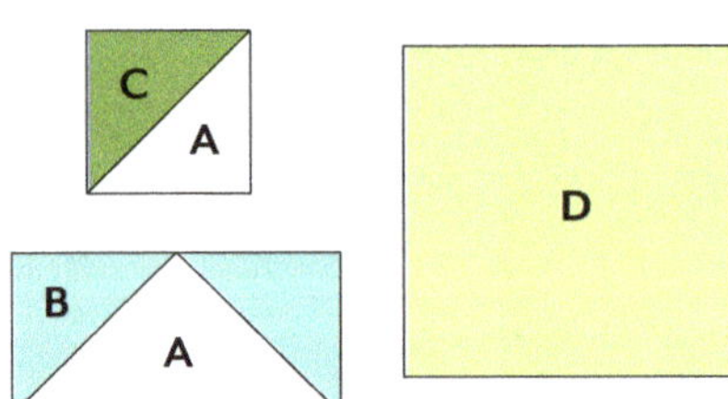

Fig. 1 Color placement

MAKE

- Four Flying Geese (p. 28) with A for the center and B for the outer triangles.
- Four Half-Square Triangle (HSTs, p. 24) in A and C.
- One 6-round Granny Square in D.

FINISHED BLOCK DIMENSIONS

YARN WEIGHT	HOOK SIZE	APPROX. BLOCK SIZE
Sport/4ply	E/4 (3.5 mm)	8¼" (21 cm)
Light Worsted/DK	G/6 (4 mm)	10" (25 cm)
Worsted/Aran	H/8 (5 mm)	12" (30 cm)
Bulky/Chunky	J/10 (6 mm)	14½" (37 cm)

Fig. 2 Seamed

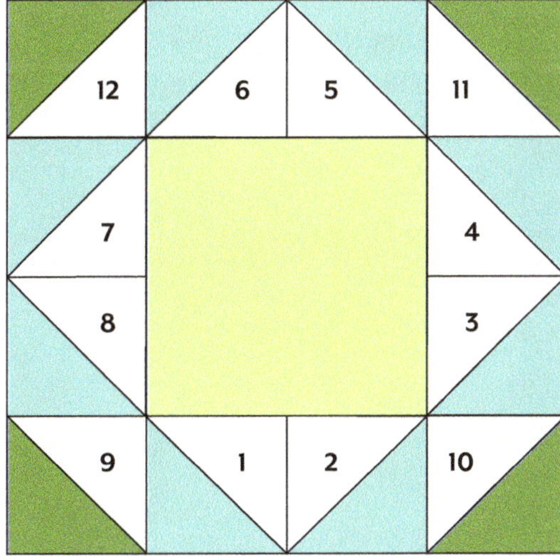

Fig. 3 JAYG

TIP It's a good idea to weave in all the ends on your individual pieces before joining. It's much easier without them in the way and saves a big task later.

ASSEMBLE

Arrange the components, following the diagram. Using your preferred joining technique (pp. 30–35), join the squares together, making the vertical seams first and then the horizontal seams (Fig. 2).

If using JAYG, as I have here, begin by making the central six-round granny square and add the four pairs of HSTs that form the flying geese around it. You will need to add these as separate HSTs. Complete the block by adding the four corner HSTs. Always begin your HST in the color you want to join with, in this case, white (A) (Fig. 3).

OPTIONAL EDGING ROUND

With the right side facing you, join your chosen yarn in any corner space. 1ch (does not count as a stitch), (1sc, 2ch, 1sc) in the same space to form a corner. 1sc in each stitch around including 1sc in each corner space where blocks join. Make (1sc, 2ch, 1sc) in the three remaining corner spaces, sl st into the first sc to join. Each side will have 44 sc, including corners. Block if required.

DUTCHMAN'S PUZZLE

The Dutchman's Puzzle quilt block dates back to the 18th century and is still a favorite with quilters today. Pairs of flying geese made in contrasting fabrics are arranged like sails on a windmill. This geometric pattern lends itself beautifully to both traditional and modern designs.

YARN

Shown in: King Cole Merino Blend DK (100% wool: 114 yd [104 m]/1.75 oz [50 g]).

Color A – Tiree

Color B – Sage

Color C – Bottle

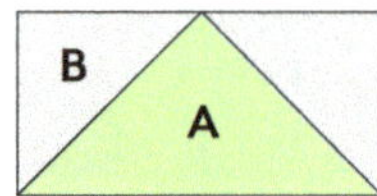

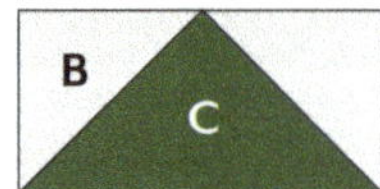

Fig. 1 Color placement

MAKE

- Four Flying Geese (p. 28) with A for the center and B for the outer triangles.
- Four Flying Geese with C for the center and B for the outer triangles.

FINISHED BLOCK DIMENSIONS

YARN WEIGHT	HOOK SIZE	APPROX. BLOCK SIZE
Sport/4ply	E/4 (3.5 mm)	8¼" (21 cm)
Light Worsted/DK	G/6 (4 mm)	10" (25 cm)
Worsted/Aran	H/8 (5 mm)	12" (30 cm)
Bulky/Chunky	J/10 (6 mm)	14½" (37 cm)

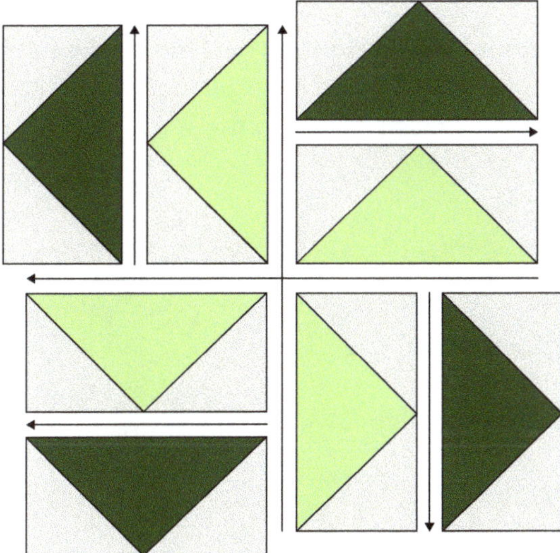

Fig. 2 Seamed

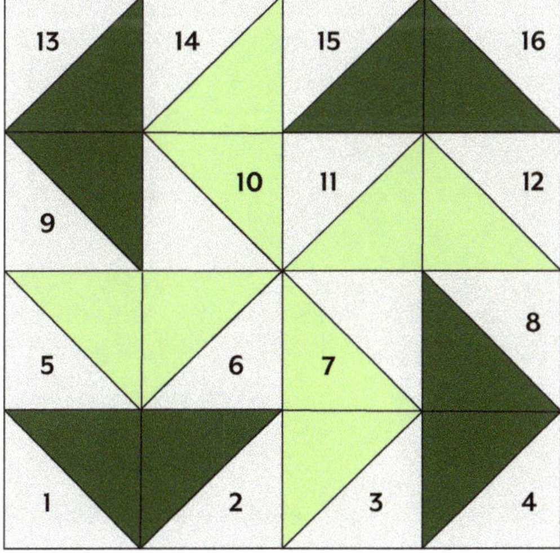

Fig. 3 JAYG

ASSEMBLE

Using your preferred joining technique (pp. 30–35), join the flying geese in pairs with the dark green at the top and the lighter green below. Then arrange the four blocks, following the diagram and join together, making the vertical seam first and then the horizontal seam (Fig. 2). For the example shown, I used whip stitch to join.

If using JAYG, you will need to make each square and add it individually, instead of making the flying geese first. Start with the bottom left hand square and work from left to right in strips. Begin making each HST in the color you want to join with, or the *first* color if you are joining two sides with different colors (Fig. 3).

OPTIONAL EDGING ROUND

With the right side facing you, join your chosen yarn in any corner space. 1ch (does not count as a stitch), (1sc, 2ch, 1sc) in the same space to form a corner. 1sc in each stitch around including 1sc in each corner space where blocks join. Make (1sc, 2ch, 1sc) in the three remaining corner spaces, sl st into the first sc to join. Each side will have 44 sc, including corners. Block if required.

CHEVRONS

The Chevron quilt block has a fresh and modern feel, but the design has a long history. Chevrons have been seen in Ancient Greek art and remained popular throughout the Middle Ages. There are as many ways to make Chevron blocks as there are centuries of use, but I have chosen a simple construction based on flying geese. Make a stylish block using two or three shades, or dive into the scrap bag for a riot of color.

YARN

Shown in: King Cole Majestic DK (50% wool, 30% acrylic, 20% polyamide: 132 yd [121 m]/1.75 oz [50 g]).

Color A – Tiree

Color B – Apple

Color C – Bayleaf

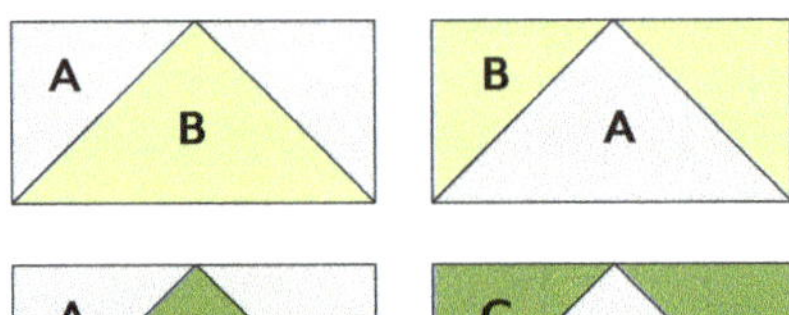

Fig. 1 Color placement

FINISHED BLOCK DIMENSIONS

YARN WEIGHT	HOOK SIZE	APPROX. BLOCK SIZE
Sport/4ply	E/4 (3.5 mm)	8¼" (21 cm)
Light Worsted/DK	G/6 (4 mm)	10" (25 cm)
Worsted/Aran	H/8 (5 mm)	12" (30 cm)
Bulky/Chunky	J/10 (6 mm)	14½" (37 cm)

Fig. 2 Seamed

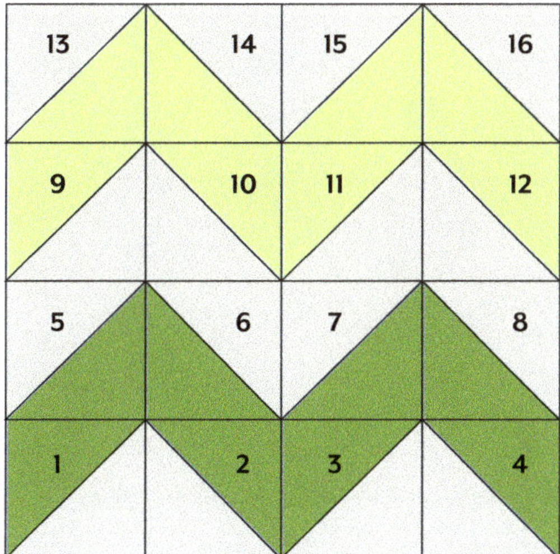

Fig. 3 JAYG

MAKE

- Two Flying Geese (pp. 30–35) with B for the center and A for the outer triangles.
- Two Flying Geese with A for the center and B for the outer triangles.
- Two Flying Geese with C for the center and A for the outer triangles.
- Two Flying Geese with A for the center and C for the outer triangles.

ASSEMBLE

Arrange the components, following the diagram. Using your preferred joining technique (pp. 30–35), join the squares together, making the vertical seam first and then the horizontal seams (Fig. 2).

If using JAYG, you will need to make each square and add it individually instead of making the Flying Geese first. Start with the bottom left hand square and work from left to right in strips. Begin making each HST in the color you want to join with or the *first* color if you are joining two sides with different colors (Fig. 3).

Weave in all ends.

OPTIONAL EDGING ROUND

With the right side facing you, join your chosen yarn in any corner space. 1ch (does not count as a stitch), (1sc, 2ch, 1sc) in the same space to form a corner. 1sc in each stitch around including 1sc in each corner space where blocks join. Make (1sc, 2ch, 1sc) in the three remaining corner spaces, sl st into the first sc to join. Each side will have 44 sc, including corners. Block if required.

BEAR PAW

The Bear Paw quilt block is named for its striking resemblance to a bear's paw with claws outstretched. The block originated in Ohio in 1823 but was seen widely across the United States with different names. In Pennsylvania, it was known as the Hand of Friendship, and the Duck's Foot in the Mud in New York. Equally at home in modern or traditional designs, I've given my Bear's Paw block a twist with bold granny stripes.

YARN

Shown in: King Cole Majestic DK (50% wool, 30% acrylic, 20% polyamide: 132 yd [121 m]/1.75 oz [50 g]).

- Color A – Cream
- Color B – Apple
- Color C – Bayleaf
- Color D – Antique
- Color E – Burnt Orange
- Color F – Rust
- Color G – Beige

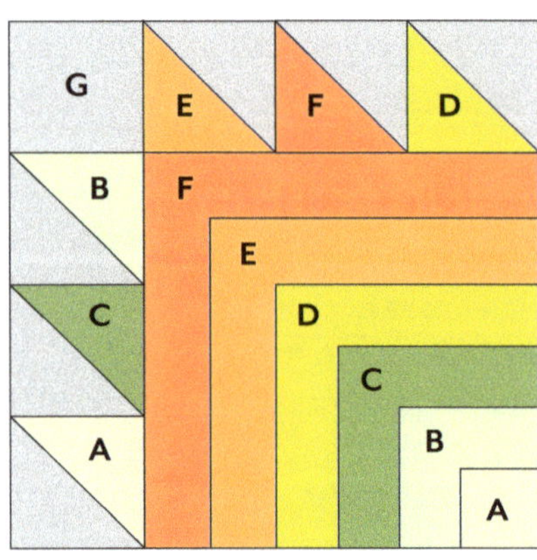

Fig. 1 Color placement

FINISHED BLOCK DIMENSIONS

YARN WEIGHT	HOOK SIZE	APPROX. BLOCK SIZE
Sport/4ply	E/4 (3.5 mm)	8¼" (21 cm)
Light Worsted/DK	G/6 (4 mm)	10" (25 cm)
Worsted/Aran	H/8 (5 mm)	12" (30 cm)
Bulky/Chunky	J/10 (6 mm)	14½" (37 cm)

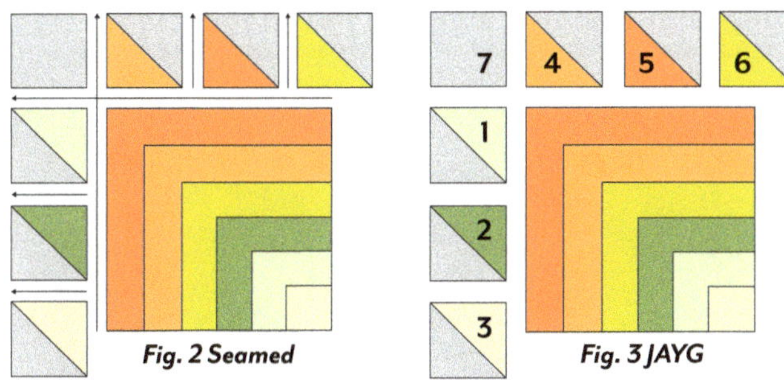

Fig. 2 Seamed

Fig. 3 JAYG

MAKE

The "Paw"

Starting with the corner square and using A, make a 2-round Granny Square (p. 22).

Row 1: Join B in any corner space. 2ch (counts as first dc here and throughout), 3dc in next space. 3dc, 2ch, 3dc in corner space. 3dc in the next space. 1dc in next corner space; leave remaining spaces unworked.

Row 2: 2ch, turn. 2dc in first space, 3dc in next 2 spaces. 3dc, 2ch, 3dc in corner space. 3dc in the next two spaces. 3dc in the last space.

Row 3: 2ch, turn. 3dc in each space to corner space. 3dc, 2ch, 3dc in corner space. 3dc in each space to last granny cluster. 1dc between the last two dc. Fasten off B.

Row 4: Join C where the previous row finished, 2ch, turn. 2dc in first space, 3dc in each space to corner space. 3dc, 2ch, 3dc in the corner space. 3dc in each space across.

Row 5: 2ch, turn. 3dc in each space to corner space. 3dc, 2ch, 3dc in the corner space. 3dc in each space to last granny cluster. 1dc between the last two dc.

Rows 6–15: Repeat Rows 4 and 5, working 1 more round with C, 3 rounds with D, 3 rounds with E, and 3 rounds with F. Fasten off and weave in ends.

The "Claws"

Make six HSTs following the colors in Fig. 1.

ASSEMBLE

Join HSTs to form two strips of three. Ensure that the "claws" are pointing in the right direction when you join them. The diagram will guide you. Join the first strip of three HSTs and the corner granny square with a continuous vertical join, followed by a horizontal join (Fig. 2).

If using JAYG, as shown, follow Fig. 2 to join your squares. For HSTs 1, 2, and 3, use color G as the background color. For HSTs 4, 5, and 6, use the reverse. This will ensure you are in the right place when you need to make your joins. Square 7 is a 3-round granny square. Add this last. Weave in all ends.

OPTIONAL EDGING ROUND

Because of how this block is constructed, it will benefit from an edging round.

With the right side facing you, join your chosen yarn in any corner space. 1ch (does not count as a stitch), (1sc, 2ch, 1sc) in the same space to form a corner. 1sc in each stitch around including 1sc in each corner space where blocks join. Make (1sc, 2ch, 1sc) in the three remaining corner spaces, sl st into the first sc to join. Each side will have 44 sc, including corners. Block if required.

LOG CABIN

The Log Cabin quilt block is a traditional design with a rich history. It features strips called logs arranged around a central square. This square often represents the heart of a home, and the logs symbolize the walls.

To create the Log Cabin block in crochet, I have used the classic technique of contrasting light and dark colors around a central square. This interesting variation of a granny square is made by rotating the square partway through rows and changing direction.

YARN

Shown in: King Cole Merino Blend DK (100% wool: 114 yd [104 m]/1.75 oz [50 g]).

- Color A – Amber
- Color B – Aran (Cream)
- Color C – Cinnamon
- Color D – Tiree
- Color E – Terracotta
- Color F – Oatmeal
- Color G – Walnut

MAKE

Using A, make a 3-round granny square (pg. 22). Place a stitch marker in the center of the right side to keep track of the front and back as you add more rows.

FINISHED BLOCK DIMENSIONS

YARN WEIGHT	HOOK SIZE	APPROX. BLOCK SIZE
Sport/4ply	E/4 (3.5 mm)	8¼" (21 cm)
Light Worsted/DK	G/6 (4 mm)	10" (25 cm)
Worsted/Aran	H/8 (5 mm)	12" (30 cm)
Bulky/Chunky	J/10 (6 mm)	14½" (37 cm)

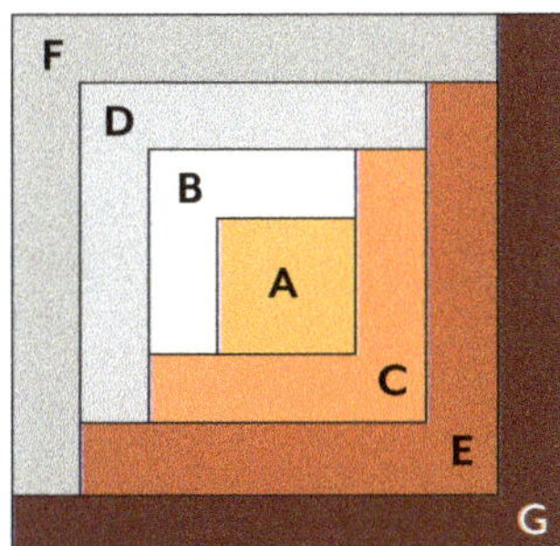

Fig. 1 Color placement

Row 1: With the wrong side facing you, join B in any corner space. 2ch (counts as the first dc here and throughout), 2dc in same corner space. 3dc in next 2 spaces. (3dc, 2ch, 3dc) in corner space. 3dc in next 3 spaces. Leave remaining spaces unworked.

Row 2: 2ch, turn. 3dc in each space to corner space. (3dc, 2ch, 3dc) in corner space. 3dc in each space to last granny cluster, 1dc in second ch of starting 2ch of previous row.

Row 3: 2ch, turn. 2dc in first space. 3dc in each space to corner space. (3dc, 2ch, 3dc) in corner space. 3dc in each space. Change to C, 2ch, and rotate work 90 degrees to the right. Complete the corner by working 3dc in the first 2ch space at the beginning of previous row. 3dc in each space to corner space. (3dc, 2ch, 3dc) in corner space. 3dc in each space across this edge of piece. 1dc in the second ch of starting 2ch of previous row.

Row 4: 2ch, turn. 2dc in first space. 3dc in each space to corner space. (3dc, 2ch, 3dc) in corner space. 3dc in each space.

Row 5: Repeat row 2.

Row 6: Change to D. 2ch and rotate work 90 degrees to the right. 2dc around dc just made at the end of previous row. 3dc in each space to corner space. (3dc, 2ch, 3dc) in corner space. 3dc in each space.

Row 7: Repeat row 2.

Row 8: Repeat row 4.

Row 9: Change to E, 2ch, and rotate work 90 degrees to the right. Complete the corner by working 3dc in the first 2ch space at the beginning of previous row. 3dc in each space to corner space. (3dc, 2ch, 3dc) in corner space. 3dc in each space. 1dc in the second ch of starting 2ch of previous row.

Row 10: Repeat row 4.

Row 11: Repeat row 2.

Row 12: Repeat row 6, this time changing to F.

Row 13: Repeat row 2.

Row 14: Repeat row 4.

Row 15: Repeat Row 9, this time changing to G.

Row 16: Repeat row 4.

Row 17: Repeat row 2.

Fasten off and weave in all ends.

OPTIONAL EDGING ROUND

An edging round will really sharpen up the appearance of this block, making joining easier, particularly where you are mixing different block types. With right side facing, join your chosen yarn in any corner space. 1ch (does not count as a stitch), (1sc, 2ch, 1sc) in the same corner space. 36sc evenly spaced along each side of the square and work (1sc, 2ch, 1sc) in the three remaining corner spaces, sl st in the first sc to join. Each side will have 38sc, including corners. Block if required.

HEART

I absolutely adore the Heart block! Those clever little HSTs genuinely shine in this wonderful design. Use a variety of shades or a single color for a truly standout piece.

YARN

Shown in: King Cole Luxury Merino DK (100% wool: 153 yd [140 m]/1.75 oz [50 g]).

Color A – Cream

Color B – Antique Rose

Color C – Vintage Rose

Color D – Dusky Rose

Color E – Carnation

Color F – Cameo

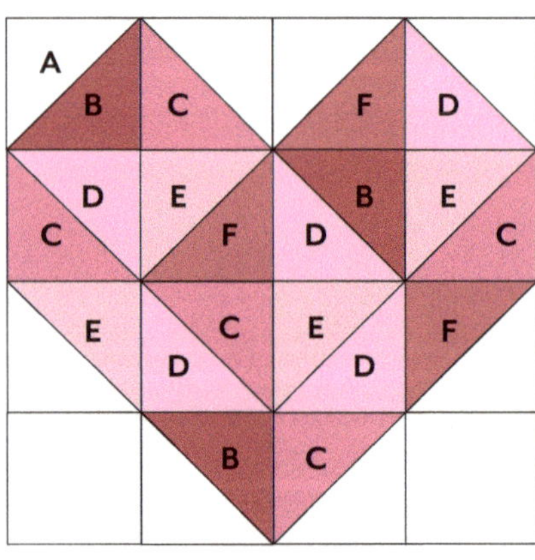

Fig. 1 Color placement

FINISHED BLOCK DIMENSIONS

YARN WEIGHT	HOOK SIZE	APPROX. BLOCK SIZE
Sport/4ply	E/4 (3.5 mm)	8¼" (21 cm)
Light Worsted/DK	G/6 (4 mm)	10" (25 cm)
Worsted/Aran	H/8 (5 mm)	12" (30 cm)
Bulky/Chunky	J/10 (6 mm)	14½" (37 cm)

Fig. 2 Seamed

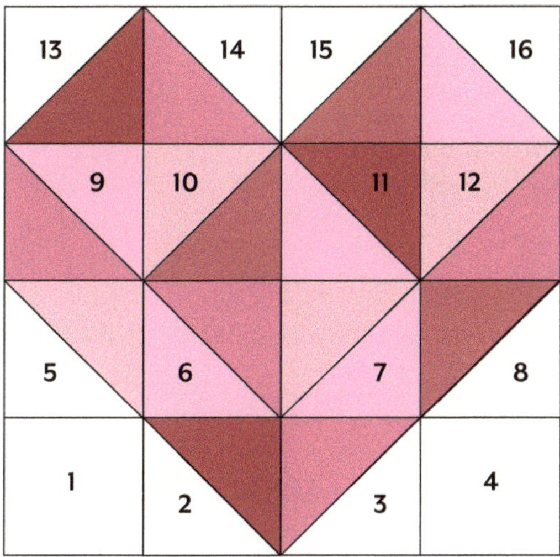

Fig. 3 JAYG

MAKE

- Fourteen HSTs, (p. 24) in the color combinations shown in Fig. 1.
- Two 3-round Granny Squares (p. 22) in A.

ASSEMBLE

Lay out your individual squares as shown in the Fig. 1. Using your preferred joining technique (pp. 30–35), make three vertical joins followed by three horizontal joins (Fig. 2).

If using JAYG, start with the bottom left corner granny square and join in the order shown in the diagram (Fig. 3). Be sure to begin making each HST in the color you want to join with or the *first* color if you are joining two sides with different colors.

OPTIONAL EDGING ROUND

With right side facing, join your chosen yarn in any corner space. 1ch (does not count as a stitch), (1sc, 2ch, 1sc) in the same corner space. 1sc in each stitch around including 1sc in each corner space where squares join and work (1sc, 2ch, 1sc) in the three remaining corner spaces, sl st in the first sc to join. Each side will have 44sc, including corners. Block if required.

SAWTOOTH STAR

The Sawtooth Star quilt block is a classic and timeless design that has been a quilter's favorite for generations. The block is constructed with a central square surrounded by triangular "teeth," radiating outward, making the design instantly recognizable. Whether used alone or combined with other blocks, the Sawtooth Star's enduring appeal lies in its simple elegance and endless design possibilities.

YARN

Shown in: King Cole Luxury Merino DK (100% wool: 153 yd [140 m]/1.75 oz [50 g]).

- Color A – Cream
- Color B – Antique Rose
- Color C – Dusky Rose

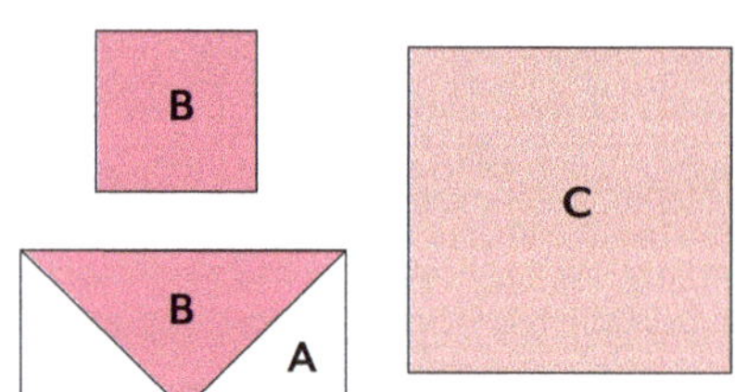

Fig. 1 Color placement

MAKE

- Four Flying Geese (p. 28) with B for the center and A for the outer triangles, as shown in Fig. 1.
- Four 3-round Granny Squares (p. 22) in B.
- One 6-round Granny Square in C.

FINISHED BLOCK DIMENSIONS

YARN WEIGHT	HOOK SIZE	APPROX. BLOCK SIZE
Sport/4ply	E/4 (3.5 mm)	8¼" (21 cm)
Light Worsted/DK	G/6 (4 mm)	10" (25 cm)
Worsted/Aran	H/8 (5 mm)	12" (30 cm)
Bulky/Chunky	J/10 (6 mm)	14½" (37 cm)

Fig. 2 Seamed

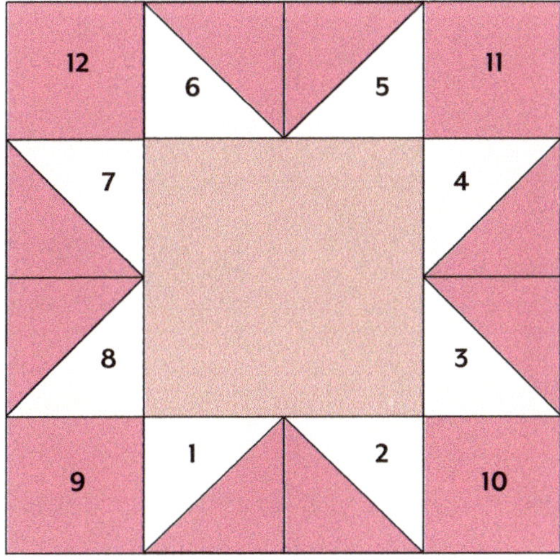

Fig. 3 JAYG

ASSEMBLE

Lay out your individual components as shown in the diagrams. Using your preferred joining technique, make two vertical joins followed by two horizontal joins (Fig. 2).

If using JAYG, as shown here, begin by making the central 6-round granny square and add the four pairs of HSTs that form the flying geese around it. Begin making each HST in the color you want to join with or the *first* color if you are joining two sides with different colors. Complete the block by adding the four corner granny squares (Fig. 3).

OPTIONAL BORDER

With right side facing, join your chosen yarn in any corner space. 1ch (does not count as a stitch), (1sc, 2ch, 1sc) in the same corner space. 1sc in each stitch around including 1sc in each corner space where squares join and work (1sc, 2ch, 1sc) in the three remaining corner spaces, sl st in the first sc to join. Each side will have 44sc, including corners. Block if required.

OHIO STAR

The Ohio Star is a classic quilt block, instantly recognizable as a patchwork design, even outside of quilting circles. It's a pretty and versatile block and fun to recreate in crochet.

YARN

Shown in: King Cole Majestic DK (50% wool, 30% acrylic, 20% polyamide: 132 yd [121 m]/1.75 oz [50 g]).

- Color A – Cream
- Color B – Pink
- Color C – Old Rose

MAKE

- Four 3-round Granny Squares (p. 22) in A.
- One 3-round Granny Square in yarn B.
- Four QSTs, (p. 26) in A and C.

Note, if you are making QSTs where more than one segment is the same color, you may need to wind a small amount of yarn from your ball separately. As a guide, each segment of a 3-round QST takes around 2¼ yards (2 m) of yarn.

FINISHED BLOCK DIMENSIONS

YARN WEIGHT	HOOK SIZE	APPROX. BLOCK SIZE
Sport/4ply	E/4 (3.5 mm)	6½" (16.5 cm)
Light Worsted/DK	G/6 (4 mm)	7½" (19 cm)
Worsted/Aran	H/8 (5 mm)	9" (23 cm)
Bulky/Chunky	J/10 (6 mm)	11" (28 cm)

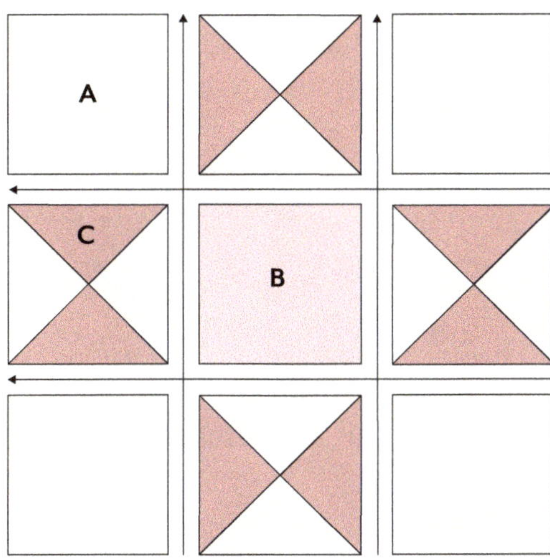

Fig. 1 Seamed

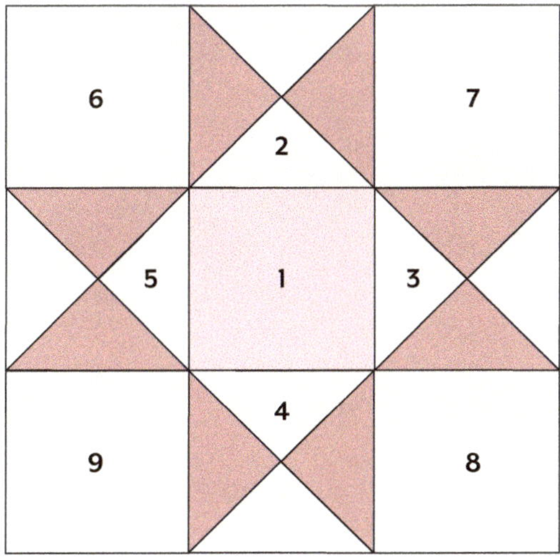

Fig. 2 JAYG

ASSEMBLE

Join the granny squares using your chosen joining technique (pp. 30–35). Make two continuous vertical joins first, followed by two horizontal joins (Fig. 1).

If using the JAYG method, start with the center square and join the four QSTs to it first. Make your joins on either of the two A sides. This will form a cross shape. Now add the four granny squares in yarn A to fill in the corner spaces (Fig. 2).

Weave in all ends.

OPTIONAL EDGING ROUND

With right side facing, join your chosen yarn in any corner space. 1ch (does not count as a stitch), (1sc, 2ch, 1sc) in the same corner space. 1sc in each stitch around including 1sc in each corner space where squares join and work (1sc, 2ch, 1sc) in the three remaining corner spaces, sl st in the first sc to join. Each side will have 33sc, including corners. Block if required.

BROKEN DISHES

The Broken Dishes quilt block is a classic design known for its simple elegance. Constructed from QSTs, the block creates a distinctive "broken" or cracked appearance. This crocheted version uses shades of a single color to highlight the effect but is also great for using up the smallest oddments of yarn.

YARN

Shown in: King Cole Majestic DK (50% wool, 30% acrylic, 20% polyamide: 132 yd [121 m]/1.75 oz [50 g]).

Color A – Berry

Color B – White

Color C – Petunia

Color D - Lilac

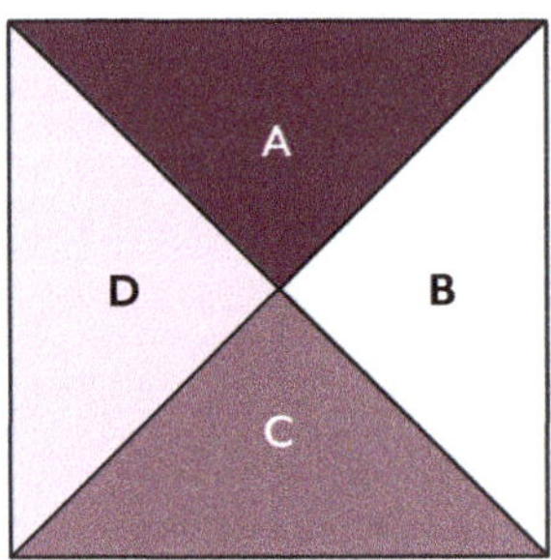

Fig. 1 Color placement

MAKE

- Nine QSTs, (p. 65) in A, B, C, and D as shown in Fig 1.

FINISHED BLOCK DIMENSIONS

YARN WEIGHT	HOOK SIZE	APPROX. BLOCK SIZE
Sport/4ply	E/4 (3.5 mm)	6½" (16 cm)
Light Worsted/DK	G/6 (4 mm)	7½" (19 cm)
Worsted/Aran	H/8 (5 mm)	9" (23 cm)
Bulky/Chunky	J/10 (6 mm)	11" (28 cm)

Fig. 2 Seamed

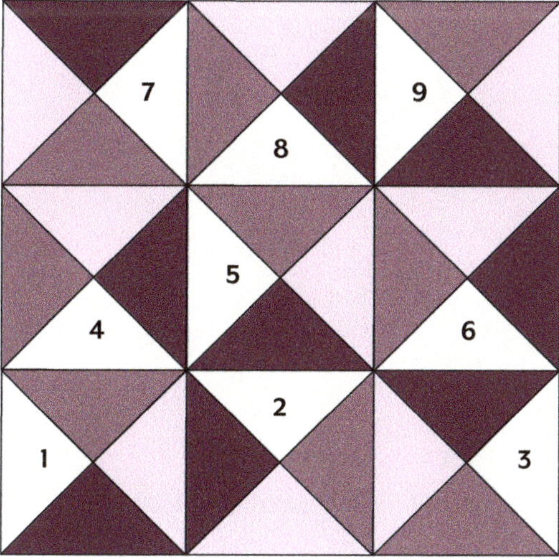

Fig. 3 JAYG

ASSEMBLE

Join using your preferred joining technique (pp. 30–35). Make two continuous vertical joins first, followed by two horizontal joins (Fig. 2).

If using JAYG, start with the first QST in the bottom left corner. Begin making each QST in the color you want to join with or the *first* color if you are joining two sides with different colors. Always work the colors in the same order, even if you don't begin with A. For instance, B, C, D, A or D, A, B, C (Fig. 3).

Weave in all ends.

OPTIONAL EDGING ROUND

With right side facing, join your chosen yarn in any corner space. 1ch (does not count as a stitch), (1sc, 2ch, 1sc) in the same corner space. 1sc in each stitch around including 1sc in each corner space where squares join and work (1sc, 2ch, 1sc) in the three remaining corner spaces, sl st in the first sc to join. Each side will have 33sc, including corners. Block if required.

DOUBLE TRAILING STAR

The Double Trailing Star quilt block uses half-square triangles (HSTs), flying geese, and classic granny squares. Instead of one, it features two stars, slightly offset, creating a sense of movement and looking deceptively complex. Combine blocks in multiple colors keep it simple with just two or three shades for a sophisticated effect.

YARN

Shown in: King Cole Merino Blend DK (100% wool: 114 yd [104 m]/1.75 oz [50 g]).

- Color A – Aran (Cream)
- Color B – Plum
- Color C – Lavender

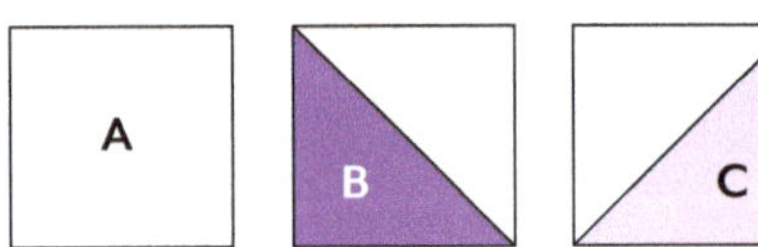

Fig. 1 Color placement

MAKE

- Eight Half-Square Triangles (HSTs, p. 24) in A and B.
- Four HSTs in A and C.
- Four 3-round Granny Squares (p. 22) in A.

FINISHED BLOCK DIMENSIONS

YARN WEIGHT	HOOK SIZE	APPROX. BLOCK SIZE
Sport/4ply	E/4 (3.5 mm)	8¼" (21 cm)
Light Worsted/DK	G/6 (4 mm)	10" (25 cm)
Worsted/Aran	H/8 (5 mm)	12" (30 cm)
Bulky/Chunky	J/10 (6 mm)	14½" (37 cm)

Fig. 2 Seamed

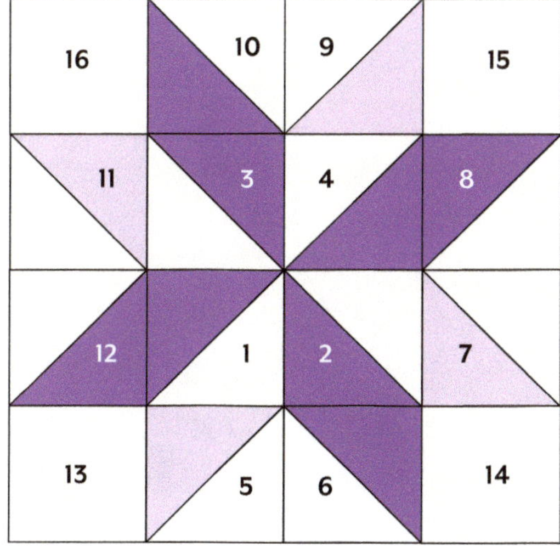

Fig. 3 JAYG

ASSEMBLE

Lay out your individual squares as shown in Fig. 1. Using your preferred joining technique (pp. 30–35), make three vertical joins followed by three horizontal joins (Fig. 2).

If using JAYG, start by joining the four central HSTs, then add pairs of HSTs to the four sides. Begin making each HST in the color you want to join with or the *first* color if you are joining two sides with different colors. Finish the block by adding the four corner granny squares (Fig. 3).

OPTIONAL BORDER

With right side facing, join your chosen yarn in any corner space. 1ch (does not count as a stitch), (1sc, 2ch, 1sc) in the same corner space. 1sc in each stitch around including 1sc in each corner space where squares join and work (1sc, 2ch, 1sc) in the three remaining corner spaces, sl st in the first sc to join. Each side will have 44sc, including corners. Block if required.

CHAPTER 3

THE PROJECTS

Now that you have mastered the blocks, it's time to start assembling them into beautiful projects. This chapter provides some inspiration for creating your own patchwork granny masterpieces. Some have a modern style, while others are classic and timeless.

Start simple with the Lavender Path Baby Blanket, or try the Exploration Sampler Blanket, showcasing all 12 blocks. Dive straight into creating an heirloom Modern Medallion Bedspread or you can create your own designs by mixing and matching blocks, exploring color palettes, and adding your own personal style. You can find helpful tips for making new layouts on page 140. The possibilities for these blocks are endless, so you can let your imagination run wild.

LAVENDER PATH BABY BLANKET

This blanket uses Nine Patch blocks (p. 42) arranged in the Irish Chain quilt pattern. Super soft merino yarn makes it perfect for a new baby, but you can make this blanket any size and with any type of yarn you like. Choose comforting chunky tweeds or zingy brights for a modern feel.

FINISHED SIZE

33½" (85 cm) wide x 45¼" (115 cm) long

YARN

Sport weight (#2 Fine)
Shown in: Drops Baby Merino (100% extra-fine merino wool: 191 yd [175 m]/1.8 oz [50g]).

Colors & Quantities

- Color A – 01 White, 10 balls
- Color B – 37 Light Lavender, 2 balls
- Color C – 53 Dew, 1 ball
- Color D – 39 Purple Orchid Mix, 1 ball
- Color E – 27 Old Pink, 1 ball
- Color F – 26 Light Old Pink, 1 ball
- Color G – 05 Light Pink, 1 ball
- Color H – 44 Powder, 1 ball

HOOKS

Size D/4 (3.5 mm)

NOTIONS

Scissors and yarn needle for weaving in ends.

NOTES

- Omit the optional edging round given in the instructions for this block.
- When making your large granny squares, remember to turn after every round to ensure they stay completely square.
- You may find that your 9-round granny squares are slightly smaller than your Nine Patch blocks. Block your squares lightly to the same dimensions before joining for the neatest finish.

Special Stitches

U.S. – Double crochet two together (dc2tog)   U.K. – Treble crochet 2 together (tr2tog)

Yarn over, insert hook in next st and pull up a loop (3 loops on hook). Yarn over, pull through 2 loops (2 loops on hook). Yarn over, insert hook in next st, pull up a loop (4loops on hook). Yarn over, pull through 2 loops (3 loops on hook), yarn over, pull through 3 remaining loops on hook.

LAVENDER PATH BABY BLANKET

INSTRUCTIONS

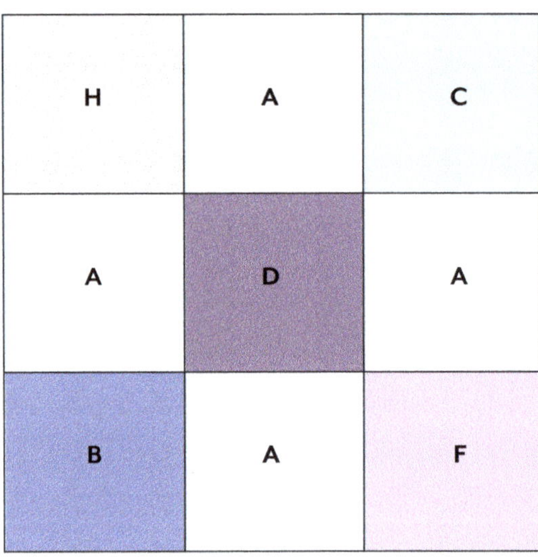

Diagram 1

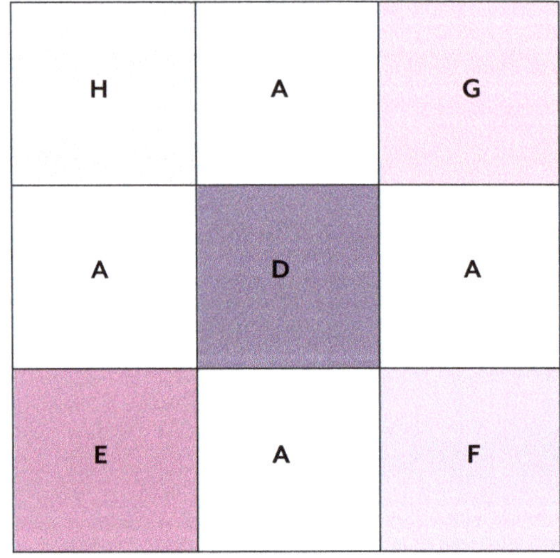

Diagram 2

MAKE BLOCKS

Using the colors show in the diagrams, or substituting your own color choices, make the following blocks:

- Twelve Nine Patch blocks (p. 42) in the blue colorway indicated on Diagram 1.
- Six Nine Patch blocks in the pink colorway indicated on Diagram 2.
- Seventeen 9-round Granny Squares in yarn A. Follow the instructions for Granny Squares (p. 22) but continue adding rounds until each side has nine sets of 3dc.

ASSEMBLE THE BLOCKS

Using yarn A and sc on the reverse side, join your blocks following the Assembly Diagram. Make the vertical joins first, from bottom to top, and then make horizontal joins from right to left. If you are left-handed, you can join from left to right.

When joining your blocks, work only in the stitches on the side of your Nine Patch blocks, and not the spaces where the individual granny squares join. This will ensure your joins line up neatly.

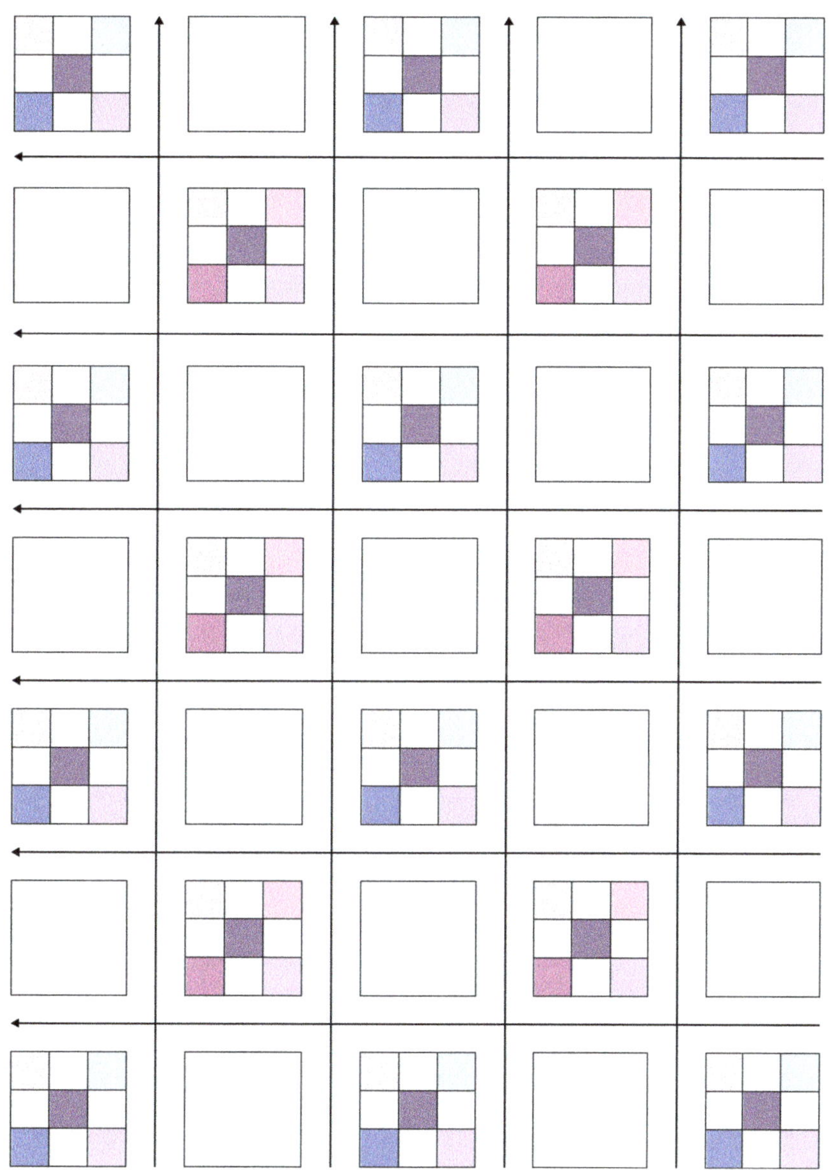

Assembly Diagram

BORDER

Round 1: With the right side facing you, join yarn A in any corner space. 2ch (counts as first dc here and throughout), 2dc in same corner space. *3dc in the next 2 spaces between clusters. 1dc in right-hand corner space where 2 squares join, dc2tog, starting in the right-hand corner space and finishing in the left-hand corner space, 1dc in the left-hand corner space,* Repeat from * to * to the next outside corner, (3dc, 2ch, 3dc) in the corner spacer. Work around in the same manner until you reach the corner you started in, 3dc in last corner space, 2ch, sl st in first dc to join.

Rounds 2–7: Turn. Sl st into corner space, 2ch, 2dc in same corner space. 3dc in each space around, working (3dc, 2ch, 3dc) in next 3 outside corner spaces until you reach the corner you started in, 3dc in the last corner space, 2ch, sl st in first dc to join. Fasten off.

Round 8: With the right side facing you, join yarn B in any corner space, 1ch, 1sc in same corner space, 1sc in each st around, working (1sc, 2ch, 1sc) in each corner space until you reach the corner you started in, 1sc in the last corner space, 2ch, sl st in first sc to join. Do not fasten off.

Round 9: Turn, sl st in the corner space, 2ch, * sl st in next st, 1dc in next st; rep from * around, working 2 sts in each corner space (in the order they appear in the alternating sl st, dc pattern), sl st in first sl st to join. There are no chains in the corners for this round. Fasten off.

FINISHING

Weave in ends. Steam block to finished size.

POLARIS SOFA THROW

Some of the most complex-looking designs can be achieved by mixing different blocks. Here, Sawtooth Star block (p. 58) and Mother's Favorite (p. 46) are tiled to achieve a striking effect. Combining these blocks makes an interesting pattern. Make sure there is plenty of contrast between your lightest and darkest shade. This adds depth and interest, so the lattice design really shines. It's a beautiful design to snuggle under on a cold night.

FINISHED SIZE

46" (117 cm) wide x 55" (140 cm) long

YARN

DK weight (#3 Light)

Shown in: King Cole Homespun DK (23% polyamide, 10% viscose, 22% wool, 23% acrylic, and 22% alpaca: 191 yd [175 m]/1.8 oz [50 g]).

Colors & Quantities

- Color A – 5109 Sea Breeze, 6 balls
- Color B – 5113 Winter Sky, 4 balls
- Color C – 5104 Midnight Sky, 6 balls
- Color D – 5106 Wild Mushroom, 3 balls

HOOKS

Size G/6 (4 mm)

NOTIONS

Scissors and yarn needle for weaving in ends.

NOTES

- This design can be easily adapted to make any size blanket you choose. Simply make more or fewer blocks to achieve the size you want. The border instructions will work on any size of blanket without any adaptations needed.

POLARIS SOFA THROW

INSTRUCTIONS

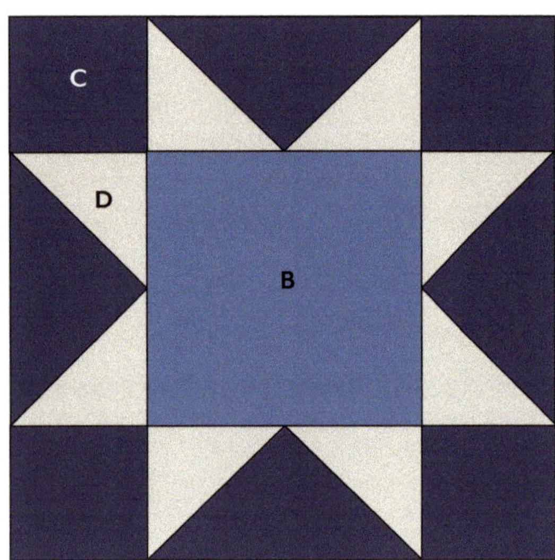

Diagram 1

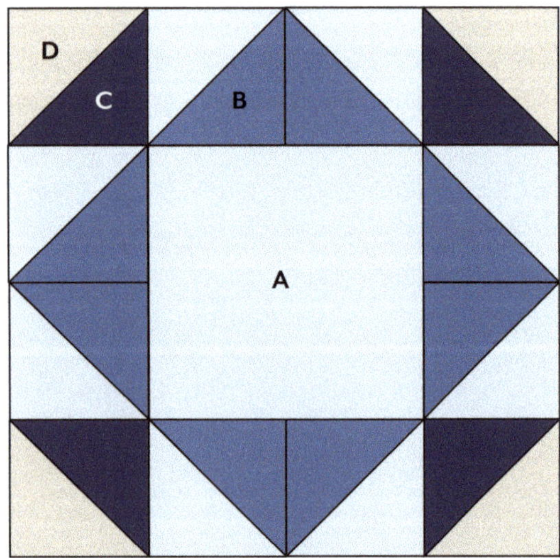

Diagram 2

MAKE THE BLOCKS

Begin by making blocks using the colors indicated on the diagrams. Make the following quantities:

- Ten Sawtooth Star blocks (p. 58) in the color combination shown in Diagram 1 with the optional sc border in C.
- Ten Mother's Favorite blocks (p. 46) in the color combination shown in Diagram 2 and the optional sc border in A.

ASSEMBLE THE BLOCKS

Working from the wrong side, use A and single crochet join (p. 32) to join your blocks following the Assembly Diagram. Make the vertical seams first then make the horizontal seams.

When joining your blocks, work through all loops of corresponding stitches and corner spaces.

Assembly Diagram

BORDER

Round 1: With the right side facing you, join A in any corner space and 1ch, (1sc, 2ch, 1sc) in same corner space. 1sc in each st and corner space where 2 blocks meet, working (1sc, 2ch, 1sc) in each corner space, sl st in first sc to join.

Round 2: 2ch (counts as first dc here and throughout), do NOT turn,1dc in each st around, working (2dc, 2ch, 2dc) in each corner space, sl st in first dc to join. Fasten off.

Round 3: With the right side facing you, join B in any corner space and 1ch, (1sc, 2ch, 1sc) in same corner space, [1ch, sk 1 st, 1sc in next st] around, working (1sc, 2ch 1sc) in each corner space, sl st in first sc to join. Fasten off.

Round 4: With the right side facing you, join yarn A in any corner space and 2ch, (1dc, 2ch, 2dc) in same corner space, 1dc in each st around, working (2dc, 2ch, 2dc) in each corner sp, sl st in first dc to join. Fasten off.

Round 5: With right side facing you, join B in any corner space and 1ch, (1sc, 2ch, 1sc) in same corner space, 1sc in each st around, working (1sc, 2ch, 1sc) in each corner space, sl st in first sc to join. Fasten off.

Round 6: With right side facing you, join C in any corner space and 2ch (counts as first hdc), (1hdc, 2ch, 2hdc) in the corner space, 1hdc in each st around, working (2hdc, 2ch, 2hdc) in each corner sp, sl st in first hdc to join. Fasten off.

FINISHING

Weave in ends. Steam block to finished size.

KALEIDOSCOPE CUSHION SET

Cushions and pillows are a great way to dip your toe into patchwork granny square projects. With this colorful set, you'll crochet Sails (p. 44) and Broken Dishes blocks (p. 62) to make throw pillows that can be adapted to suit the shape and size of the insert—just more or fewer blocks to the panel. When you're done, you'll have a splash of color perfect for any room in your home.

FINISHED SIZES

Square pillow: About 15" (38 cm) square to fit 16" (40 cm) pillow insert

Rectangle pillow: About 17" (42.5 cm) wide x 11" (27.5 cm) long x to fit 18" x 12" (45 cm x 30 cm) pillow insert

YARN

DK weight (#3 Light)
Shown in: King Cole Majestic DK (50% wool, 30% acrylic, 20% polyamide: 132 yd [121 m]/1.75 oz [50 g]).

Colors & Quantities

Square Cushion
Yarn A – White, 4 balls
Yarn B – Scraps of Apple, Pink, Lilac, Old Rose, Violet, Sky Blue, Burnt Orange, Amber, Duck Egg, Sage, Bayleaf, Rust, Antique, Cloud and Petunia (see Notes)

Rectangle Cushion
Yarn A – White, 2 balls
Yarn B – Scraps of Aran (cream), Turquoise, Slate Blue. Pale Blue, French Navy, Thyme, Sage, Amber, Redwood, Rosehip, Walnut, Raspberry, Magenta, and Lavender (see Notes)

HOOKS

Size G/6 (4 mm)

NOTIONS

Scissors, yarn needle for weaving in ends, and 16" (40 cm) square pillow insert, or 18" x 12" (45 cm x 30 cm) rectangular pillow insert

NOTES

- These cushions are a brilliant way to use up the tiniest scraps of yarn left over from other projects. I've used wool blend DK yarn; each HST requires around 2 g of yarn for each half. If you are using acrylic DK yarn, then 1.5 g will be sufficient. These quantities will be halved for each segment of the QST. A digital kitchen scale is very helpful in these situations.

- You can make a cover to suit any size or shape of cushion insert. Make one HST or QST using your chosen yarn and measure it. Now, measure your cushion and work out how many squares you will need to cover it. Ideally your cover should be about 1" (2.5 cm) smaller than the cushion pad to give a plump appearance.

KALEIDOSCOPE CUSHION SET
INSTRUCTIONS

SQUARE CUSHION

Front Panel

For the front panel, make 36 half-square triangles (HSTs, p. 24) with A and B. You can use as many or as few shades for colors B as you like. This is an excellent project for scrap yarn.

Back Panel

For the back panel, make one 18-round granny square in A. To make this, follow the instructions on page 22 for the 3-round granny square and repeat Round 3 until you have 18 rounds in total. Remember to turn after each round so your square does not start to twist.

Note: If you are making a different sized cover, your back panel needs to have as many rounds as there are sets of 3dc on each side of your front panel. I have 6 HSTs with 3 sets of 3dc each, so each side of my cover has 18 sets of 3dc. Matching up the stitch counts makes the front and back panels easy to join and gives a neat finish.

ASSEMBLE THE BLOCKS

Working from the wrong side, use yarn A and single crochet join (p. 32) to join your blocks following the Square Assembly Diagram. Make the vertical seams first then make the horizontal seams.

Block both panels to approximately 1" (2.5 cm) smaller than the insert size.

Square Assembly Diagram

JOIN THE FRONT AND BACK PANELS

Line up your front and back panels with wrong sides facing each other. With the front panel facing you, join yarn A in any corner space and 1ch, [(1sc, 2ch, 1sc) in the same corner space, 1sc in each st to next corner space] 3 times, insert your cushion pad, (1sc, 2ch, 1sc) in the next corner space, 1sc in each st to close the cover. Fasten off.

FINISHING

Weave in ends.

TIP Rather than weaving in the last tail, tuck it inside the cover. If you need to wash it, you can easily undo the top edge to remove the pad and crochet it back up afterward.

RECTANGULAR CUSHION

Front Panel

For the front panel, make 28 quarter-square triangles (QSTs, p. 24) using an assortment of colors (yarn B). For the sample shown, four similar shades were selected and arranged until I was happy with the result. Again, this is a great project to use up scraps of yarn.

Back Panel

This panel is made by working back and forth in rows. Using A, ch 67.

Row 1: 3dc in the fourth ch from hook. [sk 2ch, 3dc in next ch] to last 3 ch. sk 2ch, 1dc in last ch—21 granny clusters, a beginning 2ch, and 1 dc at end of row.

Row 2: 2ch (counts as first dc here and throughout), turn, 2dc in space between dc and first granny cluster, 3dc in each space between granny clusters across, ending with 3dc, in space between last granny cluster and beginning ch—22 granny clusters.

Row 3: 2ch, turn. 3dc in each space between granny clusters, ending with dc in top of beginning 2ch—21 granny clusters, a beginning 2ch, and 1 dc at end of row.

Rows 4–24: Repeat Rows 2 and 3, ending with a Row 2. Fasten off and weave in ends.

Note: To make a different sized rectangular panel, your foundation chain needs an additional 9 chains for every additional square you add to the width. If you have fewer squares, deduct 9 chains for every square. Work twice as many rows as you have sets of 3dc up the side of your front panel. I have 4 squares, which is 12 sets of 3dc, so I have 24 rows.

Rectangle Assembly Diagram

Block both panels to approximately 1" (2.5 cm) smaller than the insert size.

ASSEMBLE THE BLOCKS

Working from the wrong side, use A and single crochet join (p. 32) to join your blocks following the Rectangle Assembly Diagram. Make the vertical seams first then make the horizontal seams.

JOIN THE FRONT AND BACK PANELS

Line up your front and back panels with wrong sides facing each other. With the front panel facing you, join yarn A in any corner space and 1ch, [(1sc, 2ch, 1sc) in the same corner space, 1sc in each st to next corner space] 3 times, insert your cushion pad, (1sc, 2ch, 1sc) in the next corner space, 1sc in each st to close the cover. Fasten off.

FINISHING

Weave in ends.

CABIN CURRENTS BLANKET

This blanket uses the Log Cabin block (p. 54) in a bright, fresh color scheme. Rotating the blocks gives movement to this traditional design and a distinctly modern feel. Currents of warm and cool colors run diagonally for a unique visual effect.

FINISHED SIZE

41" (105 cm) wide x 53" (135 cm) long

YARN

Aran weight (#4 Medium)
Shown in: Stylecraft Special Aran (100% acrylic: 214 yd [196 m]/3.5 oz [100 g]).

Colors & Quantities

- Color A – 1035 Burgundy, 1 ball
- Color B – 1029 Copper, 1 ball
- Color C – 1711 Spice, 1 ball
- Color D – 1823 Mustard, 1 ball
- Color E – 1822 Pistachio, 1 ball
- Color F – 1820 Duck Egg, 1 ball
- Color G – 1722 Storm Blue, 1 ball
- Color H – 1019 Cloud Blue, 1 ball
- Color I – 1001 White, 1 ball
- Color J – 1005 Cream, 2 balls
- Color K – 1218 Parchment, 4 balls

HOOKS

Size H/8 (5 mm)

NOTIONS

Scissors and yarn needle for weaving in ends.

CABIN CURRENTS BLANKET

INSTRUCTIONS

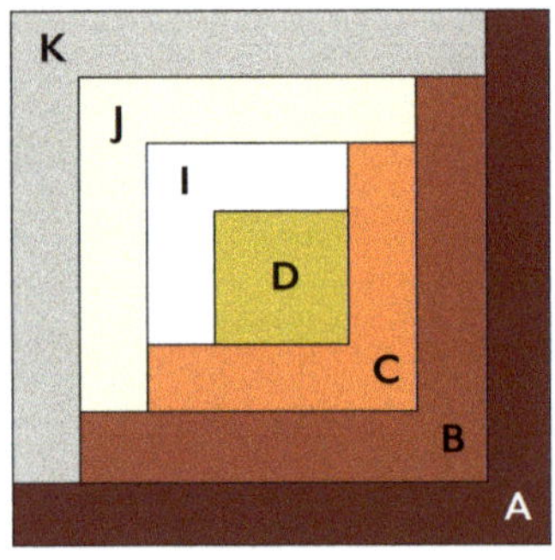

Diagram 1

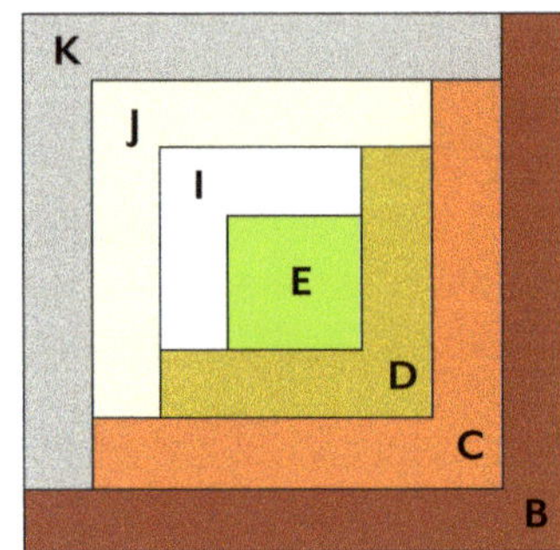

Diagram 2

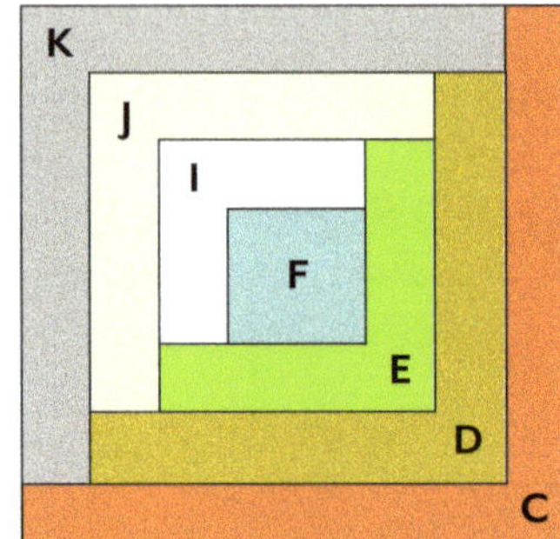

Diagram 3

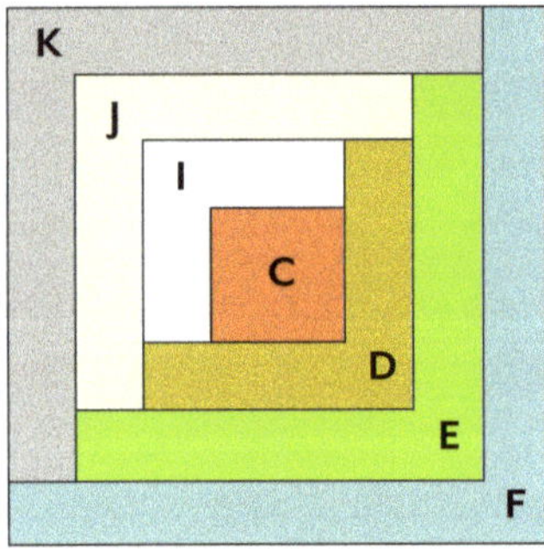

Diagram 4

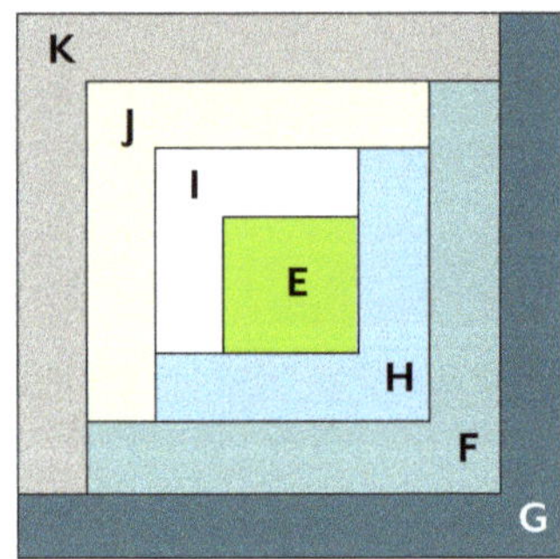

Diagram 5

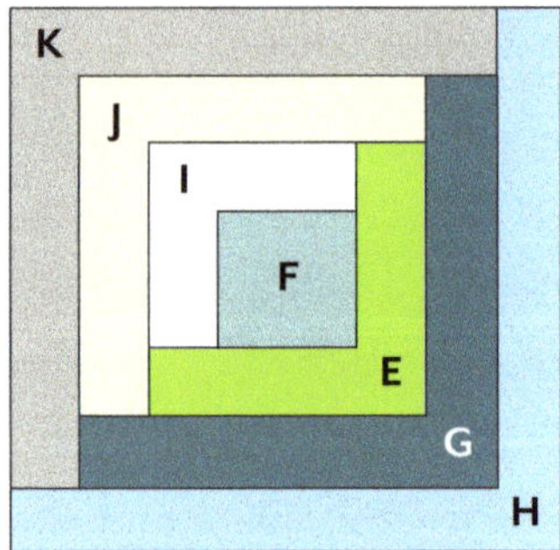

Diagram 6

MAKE THE BLOCKS

The key to the color effect of this design is strategically creating blocks with warm and cool colors, then rotating and placing them together to create the background design. You'll need to make 12 Log Cabin blocks (p. 54) total, two each of the color combinations shown in Diagrams 1–6.

Work the optional sc border in K on these blocks. Note, this edging row is ***not*** optional for this design.

ASSEMBLE THE BLOCKS

Working from the wrong side, use K and single crochet join (p. 32) to join your blocks following the Assembly Diagram. Make the vertical seams first then make the horizontal seams.

When joining your blocks, work through all loops of corresponding stitches and corner spaces.

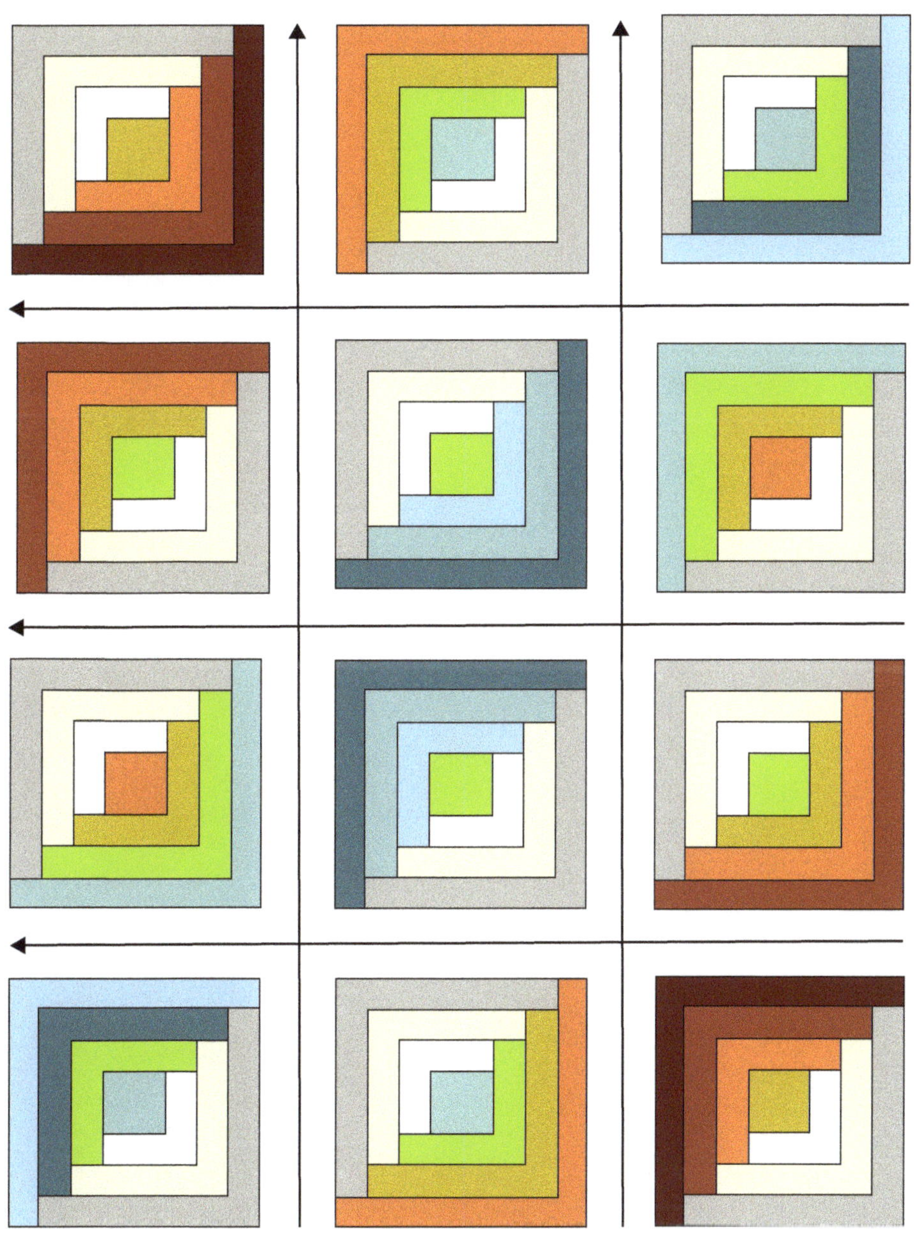

Assembly Diagram

BORDER

Round 1: With the right side facing you, join yarn K in any corner space, 2ch (counts as first dc here and throughout), (1dc, 2ch, 2dc) in the same corner space, 1dc in each st and corner space where 2 blocks meet, working (2dc, 2ch, 2dc) in each corner space, sl st in first dc to join.

Round 2: Sl st into corner space, turn. 2ch, (1dc, 2ch, 2dc) in same corner space, 1dc in each st around, working (2dc, 2ch, 2dc) in each corner space, sl st in first dc to join. Fasten off.

Round 3: With the right side facing you, join yarn C in any corner space, 1ch, (2sc, 2ch, 2sc) in the same corner space, 1sc in each st around, working (2sc, 2ch, 2sc) in each corner space, sl st in the first sc to join. Fasten off.

Rounds 4 and 5: With K repeat Rounds 1 and 2. Fasten off.

FINISHING

Weave in ends. Steam block to finished size.

KODIAK DANCE THROW

This blanket uses Bear Paw (p. 52) and Chevrons (p. 50) blocks arranged to highlight the dynamic nature of these designs. The vibrant, radial movement is achieved by creatively combining these two unique blocks and positioning their "points" toward the outer edges. This blanket would look equally at home in a modern nursery or draped over a fireside chair.

FINISHED SIZE

55" (140 cm) square

YARN

DK weight (#3 Light)
Shown in: Stylecraft Special DK (100% acrylic: 323 yd [295 m]/3.5 oz [100 g]).

Colors & Quantities

- Color A – 2171 Cinder Rose, 2 balls
- Color B – 2182 Wild Orchid, 2 balls
- Color C – 1080 Pale Rose, 1 ball
- Color D – 1218 Parchment, 1 ball
- Color E – 1820 Duck Egg, 1 ball
- Color F – 2178 North Sea, 2 balls
- Color G – 1005 Cream, 6 balls

HOOKS

Size G/6 (4 mm)

NOTIONS

Scissors and yarn needle for weaving in ends.

NOTES

- The individual blocks in the sample shown were made using the JAYG method (p. 34). Then, finished blocks were joined using single crochet seams on the reverse (p.32).

Special Stitch

U.S. – Double crochet two together (dc2tog)   U.K. – Treble crochet 2 together (tr2tog)

Yarn over, insert hook in next st and pull up a loop (3 loops on hook). Yarn over, pull through 2 loops (2 loops on hook). Yarn over, insert hook in next st, pull up a loop (4loops on hook). Yarn over, pull through 2 loops (3 loops on hook), yarn over, pull through 3 remaining loops on hook.

KODIAK DANCE THROW
INSTRUCTIONS

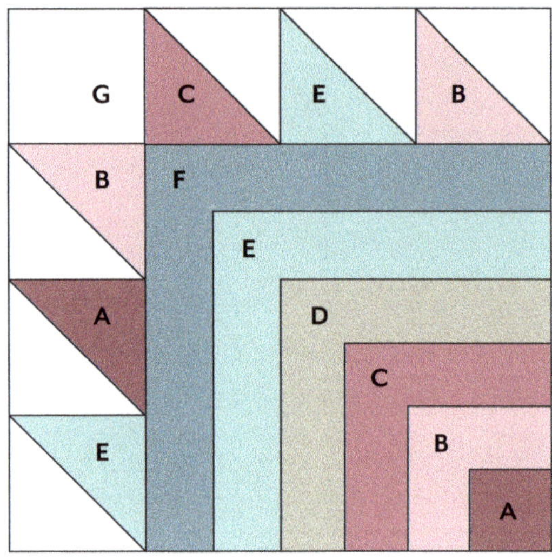

Diagram 1

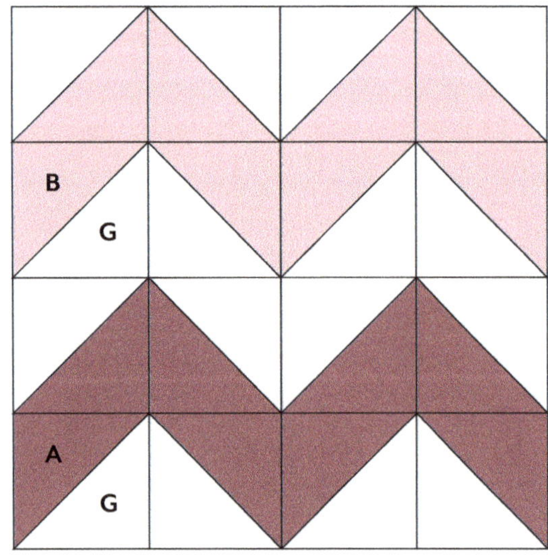

Diagram 2

MAKE THE BLOCKS

Begin by making 8 Bear Paw blocks (p. 52) using the color placement shown in Diagram 1. Then, make 8 Chevrons blocks (p. 50) using the color placement shown in Diagram 2.

Omit the optional edging given in the instructions for these blocks and add the following instead. This alternative edging will give the effect of sashing in the finished throw.

Block Edging

Round 1: With the right side facing you, join G in any corner space. 2ch (counts as first dc here and throughout), 2dc in same corner space. *3dc in the next 2 spaces. 1dc in right-hand corner space where 2 squares join, dc2tog, starting in the right-hand corner space and finishing in the left-hand corner space, 1dc in the left-hand corner space.* Repeat from * to * until you reach the next outside corner, (3dc, 2ch, 3dc) in the corner spacer. Work around in the same manner until you reach the corner you started in. 3dc in last corner space, 2ch, sl st in first dc to join.

Rounds 2 and 3: Turn. Sl st into corner space, 2ch, 2dc in same corner space. 3dc in each space around, working (3dc, 2ch, 3dc) in next 3 outside corner spaces until you reach the corner you started in, 3dc in the last corner space, 2ch, sl st in first dc to join. Fasten off.

ASSEMBLE THE BLOCKS

Working from the wrong side, use yarn G and single crochet join (p. 32) to join your blocks following the Assembly Diagram. Make the vertical seams first then make the horizontal seams.

When joining your blocks, work through all loops of corresponding stitches and corner spaces.

Assembly Diagram

BORDER

Round 1: With the wrong side facing you, join yarn G in any corner space. 2ch (counts as first dc here and throughout), 2dc in same corner space. *3dc in each space to next corner space where 2 squares join, 1dc in right hand corner space where 2 squares join, dc2tog, starting in the right-hand corner space and finishing in the left-hand corner space 1dc in the left-hand corner space.* Repeat from * to * until you reach the next outside corner, (3dc, 2ch, 3dc) in the corner space. Work around in the same manner until you reach the corner you started in. 3dc in last corner space, 2ch, sl st in first dc to join.

Rounds 2 and 3: Sl st into corner space, turn, 2ch, 2dc in same corner space. 3dc in each space around, working (3dc, 2ch, 3dc) in next 3 outside corner spaces until you reach the corner you started in, 3dc in the last corner space, 2ch, sl st in first dc to join.

Rounds 4–6: Change to F and repeat Round 2 three more times. Fasten off.

Round 7: With the right side facing you, join yarn E in any corner space. 2ch (counts as first hdc), (1hdc, 2ch, 2hdc) in the same corner space, 1hdc in each st around, working (2hdc, 2ch, 2hdc) in each corner space, sl st under both loops of first hdc to join. Fasten off.

FINISHING

Weave in ends. Steam block to finished size.

FIRST FROST BLANKET

The repetition of this simple star design on a crisp white background gives this blanket a frosty winter feel. However, this design would suit any combination of colors. I've used worsted yarn, but this would make a pretty baby blanket in a finer weight yarn.

FINISHED SIZE

55" (140 cm) square

YARN

Worsted weight (#4 Medium)

Shown in: Knit Picks/WeCrochet Heatherly Worsted (80% acrylic, 20% merino wool: 218 yd [199 m]/3.5 oz [100 g]).

Colors & Quantities

- Color A – Snowflake, 10 hanks
- Color B – Cabana, 1 hank
- Color C – Seaglass, 1 hank
- Color D – Agave, 1 hank
- Color E – Sweet Bing, 1 hank
- Color F – Fairy Cottage, 1 hank

HOOK

Size H/8 (5 mm)

NOTIONS

Scissors and yarn needle for weaving in ends.

NOTES

- You can adapt this pattern to make any size blanket you choose. The border instructions will work without any adaptations needed.

FIRST FROST BLANKET

INSTRUCTIONS

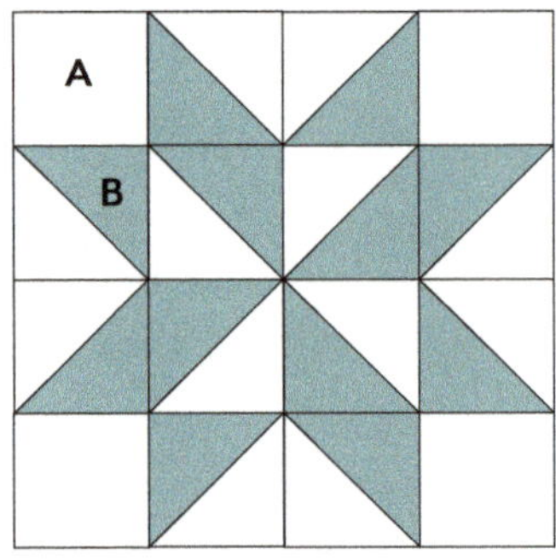

Diagram 1 Make 4

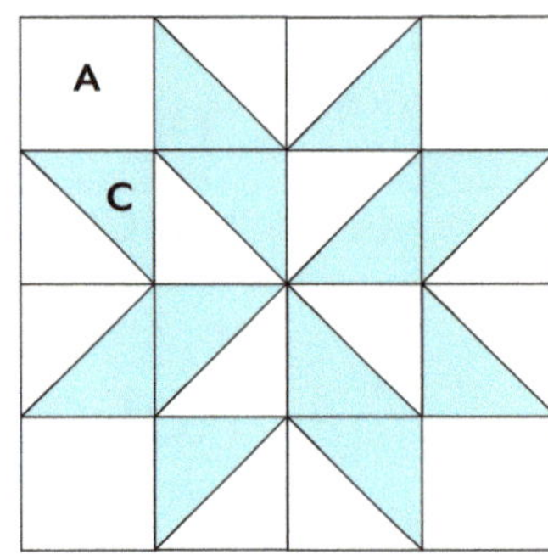

Diagram 2 Make 4

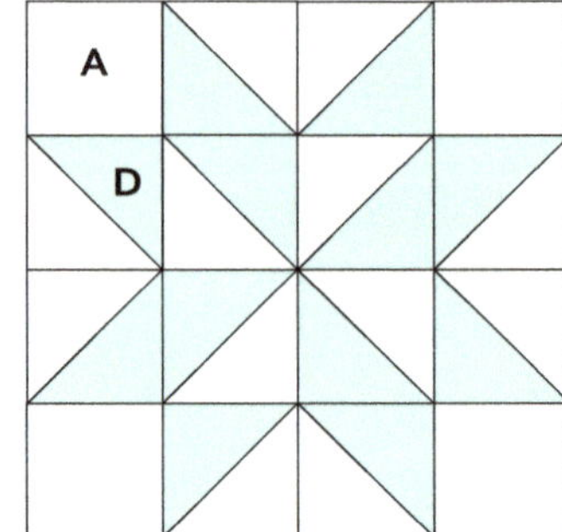

Diagram 3 Make 3

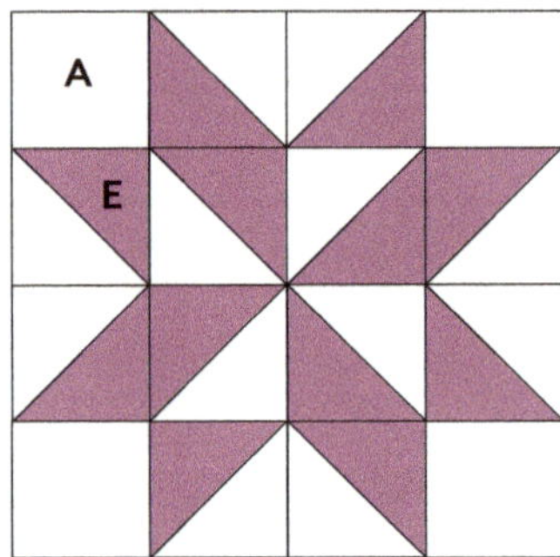

Diagram 4 Make 3

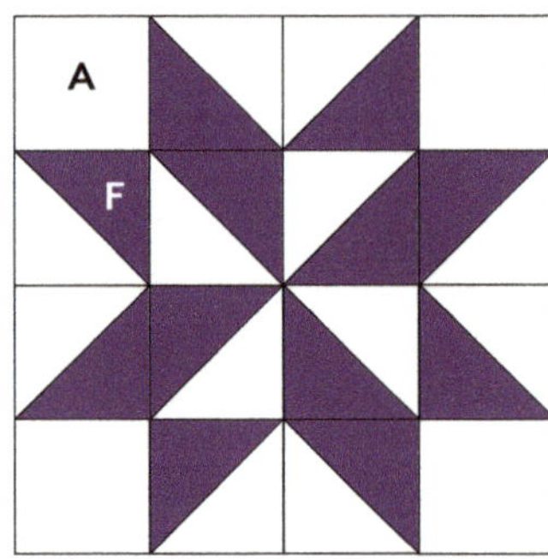

Diagram 5 Make 3

MAKE THE BLOCKS

This blanket design used the Double Trailing Star block (p. 64) using different colors for contrast color. Use the instructions to create blocks with the following color combinations:

- Three blocks using A and B, Diagram 1.
- Four blocks using A and C, Diagram 2.
- Three blocks using A and D, Diagram 3.
- Three blocks using A and E, Diagram 4.
- Three blocks using A and F, Diagram 5.

You should have 16 Double Trailing Star blocks in total.

JOIN THE BLOCKS

Working from the wrong side, use A and single crochet join (p. 32) to join your blocks following the Assembly Diagram. Make the vertical seams first then make the horizontal seams.

When joining your blocks, work through all loops of corresponding stitches and corner spaces.

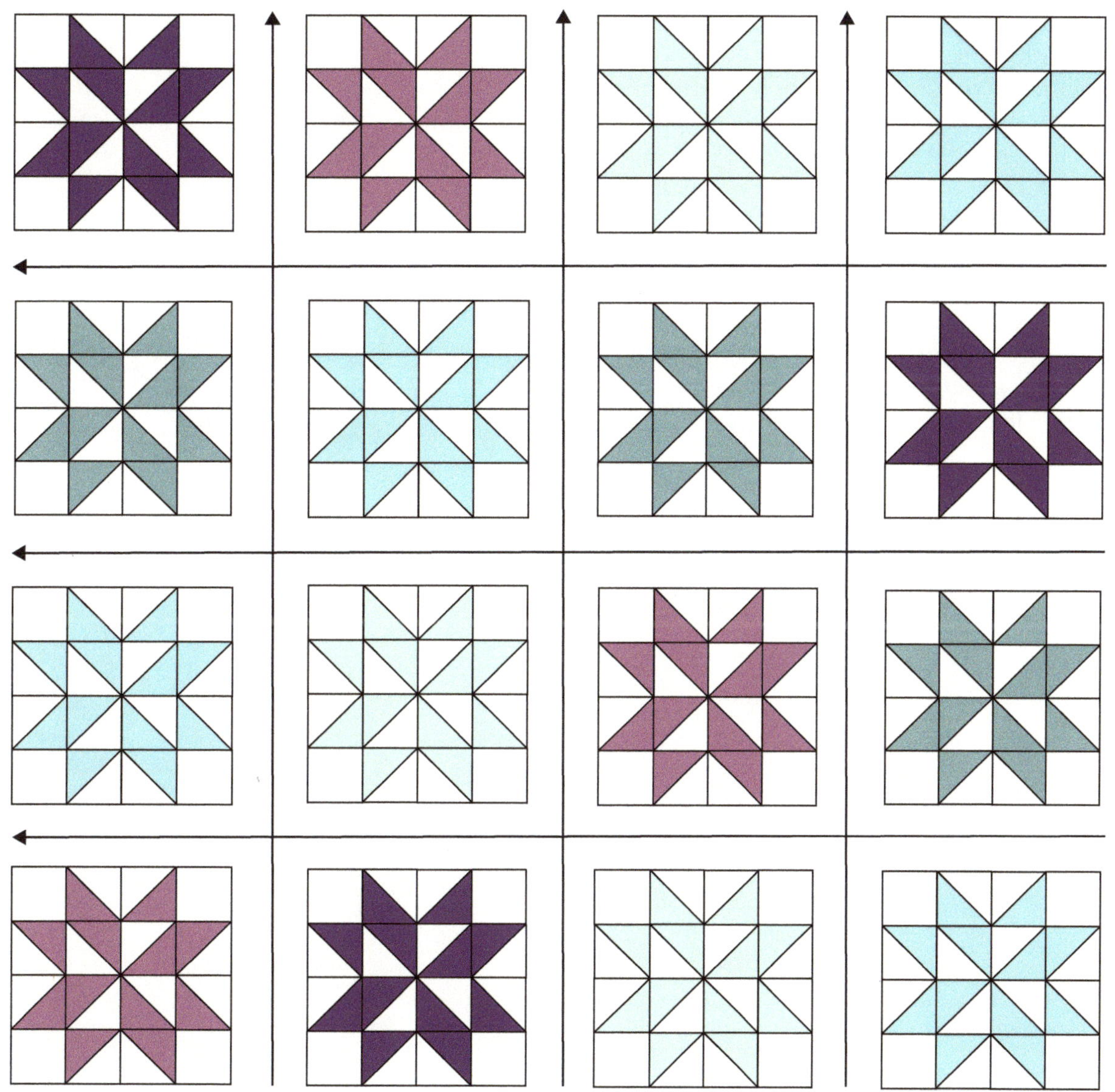

Assembly Diagram

BORDER

Round 1: With the right side facing you, join yarn A in any corner space and 2ch (counts as first dc here and throughout), (1dc, 2ch, 2dc) in same corner space, 1dc in each st and corner space where 2 blocks meet, working (2dc, 2ch, 2dc) in each corner space, sl st in first dc to join. Fasten off.

Round 2: With the wrong side facing you, join yarn B in any corner space and 2ch, (1dc, 2ch, 2dc) in same corner space, 1dc in each st and corner space where 2 blocks meet, working (2dc, 2ch, 2dc) in each corner space, sl st in first dc to join. Fasten off.

Round 3: With the right side facing you, join yarn A in any corner space and 1ch, (1sc, 2ch, 1sc) in same corner space, 1sc in each st around, working (1sc, 2ch 1sc) in each corner space, sl st in first sc to join. Fasten off.

FINISHING

Weave in ends. Steam block to finished size.

EXPLORATION SAMPLER BLANKET

Sampler quilts are a traditional way to show off a variety of blocks rather than one or two blocks repeating. In this design, I have included all 12 blocks featured in this book to create a modern crochet version of a sampler blanket.

FINISHED SIZE

43¼" (110 cm) wide x 57" (145 cm) long

YARN

DK weight (#3 Light)

Shown in: The Grey Sheep Co. Hampshire DK (100% virgin British wool: 136 yd [125 m]/1.75 oz [50 g]).

Colors & Quantities

- Color A – A Little of What You Fancy, 1 hank
- Color B – Berry, 1 hank
- Color C – Reputation, What Reputation?, 1 hank
- Color D – A Friendly Girl, 1 hank
- Color E – Looking in the Mirror, 1 hank
- Color F – Compromised, 1 hank
- Color G – Dragon Glass, 1 hank
- Color H – The Perfect Storm, 1 hank
- Color I – Barafundle Bay, 1 hank
- Color J – Acid Rain, 1 hank
- Color K – Under the Old Oak, 1 hank
- Color L – Oatmeal, 6 hanks
- Color M – Naturally, 2 hanks
- Color N – Mouse in the House, 2 hanks

HOOKS

Size G/6 (4 mm)

NOTIONS

Scissors and yarn needle for weaving in ends.

NOTES

- The sampler shown was made using JAYG for the blocks and then the finished blocks were joined using single crochet seams on the wrong side. However, this will work with any of the joining methods, so you can choose what you prefer.
- Take care to read through and work the edging rounds required for each block.
- If you would like to make a larger blanket, I suggest experimenting with different HST layouts to make panels around the outer edge before starting the border.
- The border will work for any size blanket.
- I've chosen a palette of exquisite 100% wool yarn from sheep reared in the British countryside, but this would make a fabulous stash buster.

EXPLORATION SAMPLER BLANKET

INSTRUCTIONS

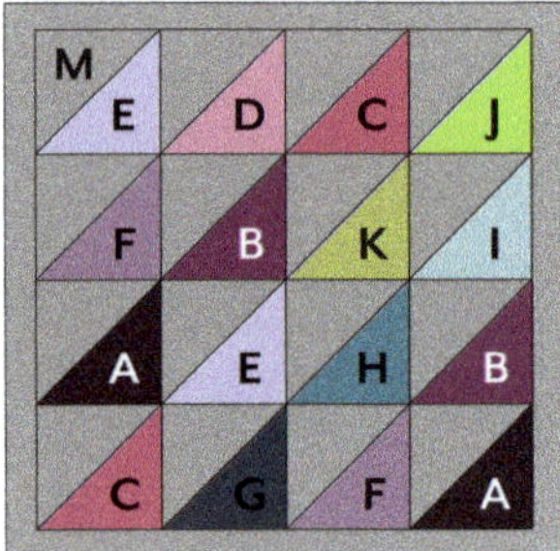

Diagram 1 Sails

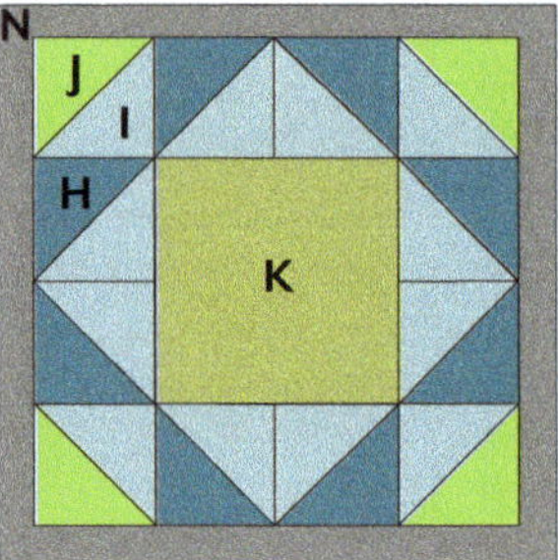

Diagram 2 Mother's Favorite

Diagram 3 Dutchman's Puzzle

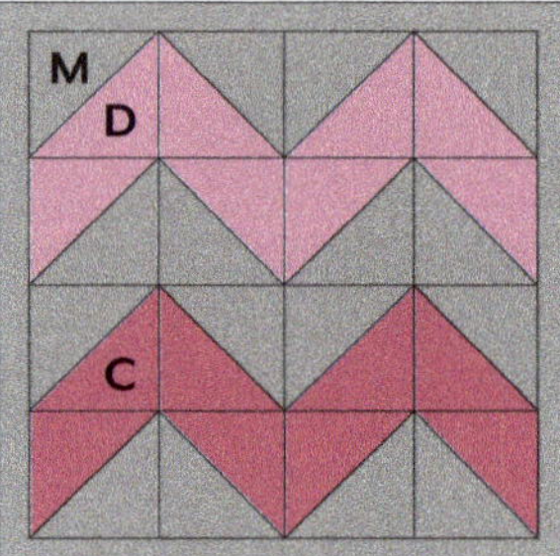

Diagram 4 Chevrons

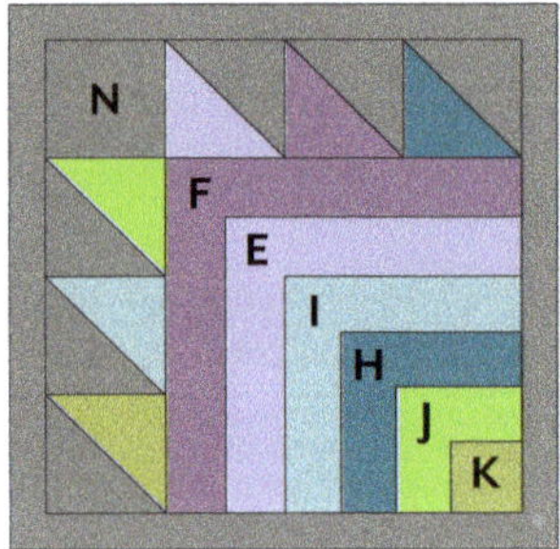

Diagram 5 Bear Paw

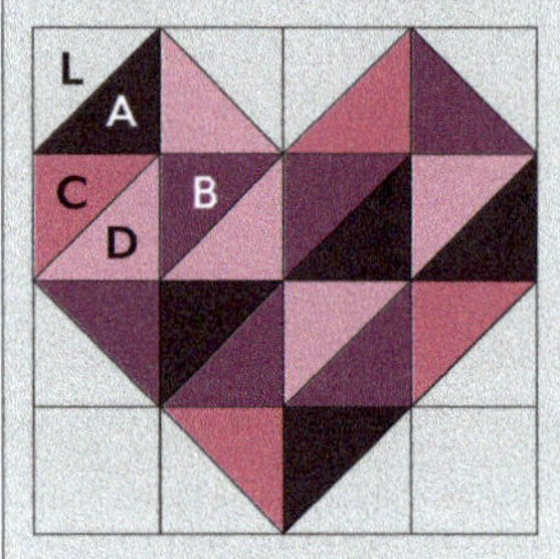

Diagram 6 Heart

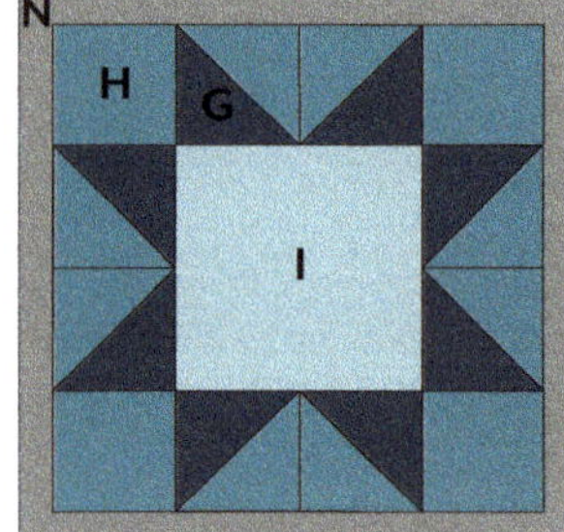

Diagram 7 Sawtooth Star

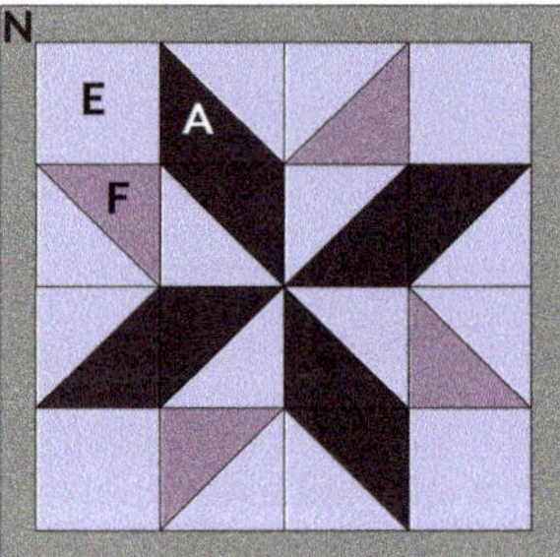

Diagram 8 Double Trailing Star

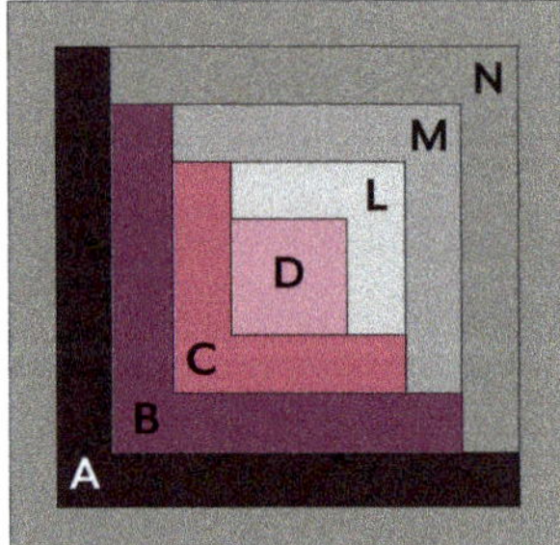

Diagram 9 Log Cabin

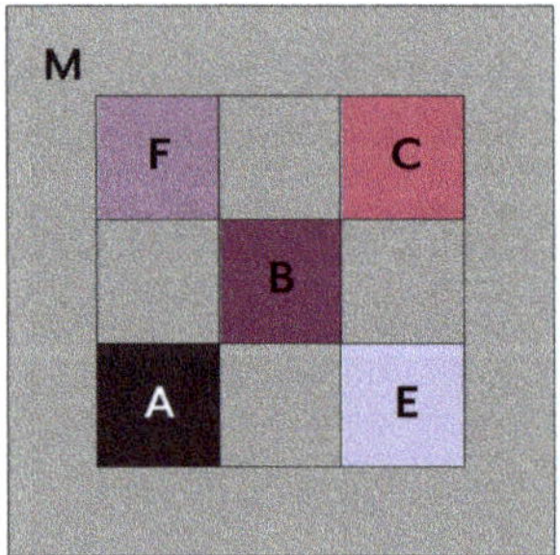

Diagram 10 Nine Patch

Diagram 11 Ohio Star

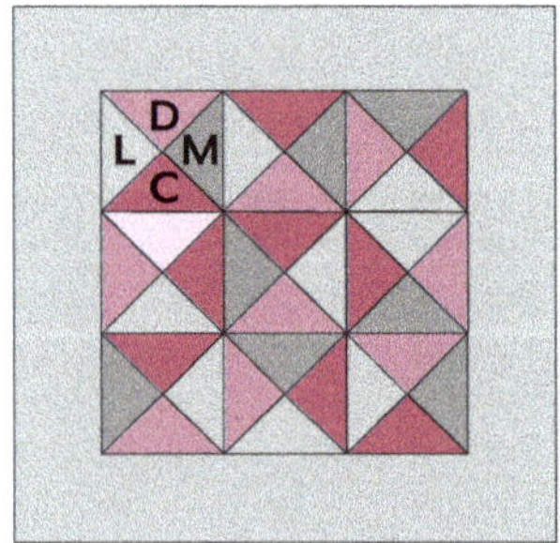

Diagram 12 Broken Dishes

MAKE THE BLOCKS

Blocks 1–8

To make the various blocks fit together properly, they need to be the same finished size. To achieve this, some blocks have a slightly different edging treatment before they are joined. You'll be crocheting one each of the following eight blocks on pages 40–64 in the colors noted. Omit the optional edging round given in the block instructions and work the following instead.

Make one each of the following:

- Sails, using A, B, C, D, E, F, G, H, I, and M, and Diagram 1.
- Mother's Favorite, using H, I, J, K, and N, and Diagram 2.
- Dutchman's Puzzle, using J, K, and L, and Diagram 3.
- Chevrons, using C, D, and M, and Diagram 4.
- Bear Paw, using E, F, H, I, J, K, and N, and Diagram 5.
- Heart, using A, B, C, D, and L, and Diagram 6.
- Sawtooth Star, using G, H, I, and N, and Diagram 7.
- Double Trailing Star, using A, E, F, and N, and Diagram 8.

These eight blocks all have the same edging.

Edging Round 1: With the right side facing you, join the edge color shown in the block's respective diagram in any corner space. 1ch (does not count as a stitch), 1sc, 2ch, 1sc in same space to form a corner. 1sc in each stitch around, including 1sc in each corner space where blocks join. Make 1sc, 2ch, 1sc in the three remaining corner spaces, sl st in first sc to join. Each side will have 44 sc, including corners.

Edging Round 2: Sl st into first corner space. 2ch (counts as first dc here and throughout), (1dc, 2ch, 1dc) in the same corner space,1dc in each st around, working (1dc, 2ch, 1dc) in each corner space, sl st in first dc to join. Each side will have 46 dc. Fasten off.

Block 9

Next, make one Log Cabin block using colors A, B, C, D, L, M, and N, and Diagram 9.

This block has a slightly different edging to bring the stitch count in line with the other blocks.

Edging Round 1: With the right side facing you, join the edge color indicated in Diagram 9 in any corner space, 1ch, (2sc, 2ch, 2sc) in same corner space, 1sc in each st around, working (2sc, 2ch, 2sc) in each corner space, sl st in first sc to join. Fasten off. Each side will have 40 sc.

Edging Rounds 2–3: Sl st into corner space, turn, 2ch (counts as first dc here and throughout), (1dc, 2ch, 2dc) in the same corner space, 1dc in each st around, working (2dc, 2ch, 2dc) in each corner space, sl st under both loops of first dc to join. Fasten off. Each side will have 46 dc in Round 3.

Blocks 10–12

Finally, make one of each of the following:

- Nine Patch, using A, B, C, E, F, and M, and Diagram 10.
- Ohio Star, using G, H, and L, and Diagram 11.
- Broken Dishes, C, D, L, and M, and Diagram 12.

These three blocks have additional edging rounds to make them the same size and stitch count as the other nine. Omit the optional edging rounds given in the instructions for these blocks and work the following instead. The yarn shade for edging is shown on the block color illustrations.

Edging Round 1: With the right side facing you, join the edge color shown in the block's respective diagram in any corner space. 2ch (counts as first dc here and throughout), (1dc, 2ch, 1dc) in the same corner space, 1dc in each st around, working (2dc, 2ch, 1dc) in each corner space, sl st in first dc to join. Fasten off. Each side will have 34 dc.

Edging Rounds 2–4: Sl st into corner space, turn, 2ch, (1dc, 2ch, 2dc) in the same corner, 1dc in each stitch around, working (2dc, 2ch, 2dc) in each corner space, sl st under both loop of first dc to join. Fasten off. Each side will have 46 dc in Round 4.

ASSEMBLE THE BLOCKS

Working from the wrong side, use L and single crochet join to join your blocks following the Assembly Diagram. Make the vertical seams first then make the horizontal seams.

When joining your blocks, work through all loops of corresponding stitches and corner spaces.

Assembly Diagram

BORDER

Round 1: With the right side facing you, join L in any corner space. 2 ch (counts as first dc here and throughout), (1dc, 2ch, 1dc) in the same corner space, 1dc in each stitch around, working (2dc, 2ch, 1dc) in each corner space, sl st in first dc to join.

Rounds 2–4: Sl st into corner space, turn, 2ch (counts as first dc), (1dc, 2ch, 2dc) in the same corner space, 1dc in each st around, working (2dc, 2ch, 2dc) in each corner space, sl st in first dc to join.

Round 5: Sl st into corner space, turn, 4ch (counts as 1dc and 2ch), 1dc in same corner space, * 1ch, sk 1dc, 1dc * Repeat from * to * around, working (1dc, 2ch 1dc) in each corner, sl st in the 2nd ch of the starting 4ch to join.

Rounds 6–9: Sl st into corner space, turn, 2ch, (1dc, 2ch, 2dc) in the same corner space, 1dc in each stitch around, working (2dc, 2ch, 2dc) in each corner space, sl st in first dc to join. Fasten off.

Round 10: With the right side facing you, join A in any corner space, 1ch, (2sc, 2ch, 2sc) in same corner space, 1sc in each stitch around, working (2sc, 2ch, 2sc) in each corner space, sl st in first sc to join. Fasten off.

FINISHING

Weave in ends. Steam block to finished size.

FIRESIDE BLANKET

Perfectly sized to wrap around your shoulders while enjoying the warmth of a campfire, the Fireside Blanket combines traditional quilt blocks with modern, ember-toned yarn and a chunky ribbed edging.

FINISHED SIZE

42" (107 cm) wide x 58¾" (147cm) long

YARN

Aran weight (#4 Medium)
Shown in: (A) Sirdar Jewelspun Aran (100% acrylic: 547 yds [500 m]/7 oz [200 g]).
(B) Sirdar Hayfield Bonus Aran with wool (80% acrylic, 20% wool: 920 yd [840 m]/14 oz [400 g]).

Colors & Quantities

Yarn A – 855 Sunstone Amber, 2 balls

Yarn B – 813 Croft Gray, 2 balls

HOOKS

Size H/8 (5 mm)
Size 7 (4.5 mm), for ribbed edging only

NOTIONS

Scissors and yarn needle for weaving in ends.

NOTES

- If you are using Sirdar Jewelspun Aran, or a similar variegated yarn, join the blocks in the order you make them. This will preserve the gradient effect of the yarn.
- Crochet ribbing tends to curl, but you can easily remedy this by blocking. I find blasting with steam and gently easing it to lay flat while warm does the trick.
- This blanket is made in five horizontal panels with crochet in rows to represent sashing. The panels are then joined using single crochet and finished with a ribbed edge.

Special Stitches

U.S. - Front post double crochet (fpdc) U.K. - Front post treble crochet (fptc)

Yarn over and insert hook underneath the dc two rows below. Pull up a loop.
Yarn over and pull through two loops. Yarn over and pull through remaining two loops.

FIRESIDE BLANKET

INSTRUCTIONS

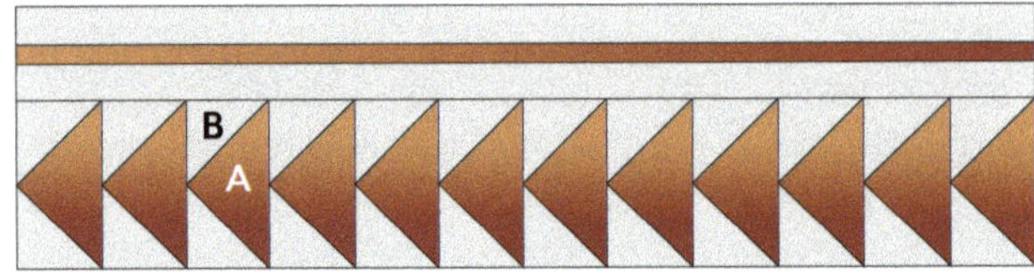

Panel One

PANEL ONE

Using the larger hook, make 12 flying geese (p. 28). Use A in the center and B on the outside. Join using sc on the wrong to form a strip.

Sashing Row 1: With the right side facing you and flying geese pointing to the left, join yarn B in the top right corner space of first flying geese block. 2ch (counts as first dc here and throughout), 1dc in each st across, including the corner spaces where blocks join. [132dc].

Sashing Row 2: 2ch, turn. 1dc in first st and in each st across. [133dc].

Sashing Row 3: 2ch, turn, 1dc in first st, *sk 2 sts, 3dc in next st* Repeat from * to * to last 3 sts, sk 2 sts, 2dc in last st. [43 3-dc clusters and two 2-dc clusters].

Sashing Row 4: Change to A, 2ch, turn, 3dc in each space between clusters, 1dc between the last 2 dc. [44 3-dc clusters].

Sashing Row 5: Change to B, 2ch, turn, 1dc in first space between clusters. 3dc in each space between clusters to last space, 2dc in last space.

Sashing Row 6: 2ch, turn. 1dc in each st across. [133dc].

Sashing Row 7: 2ch, 1dc in each st to last 2sts, sk 1 st, 1dc in last st. Fasten off. [132dc].

Panel Two

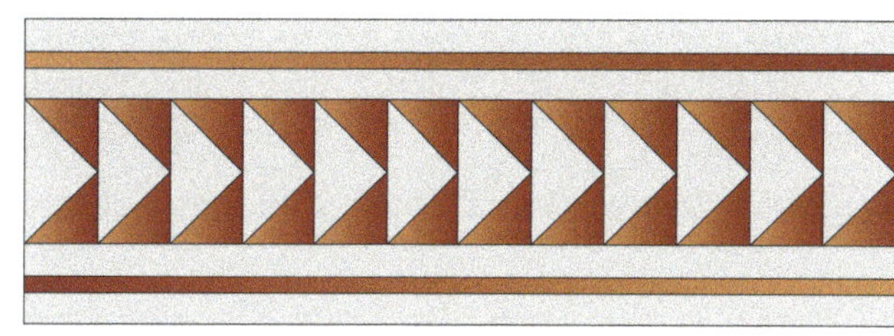

Panel Three

PANEL TWO

Make four Ohio Star blocks (p. 60), as shown in Panel Two. Use single crochet join to join the individual squares within the blocks. Join the blocks using single crochet join worked on the wrong side to form a strip.

PANEL THREE

Make 12 flying geese (p. 28) using B in the center and A on the outside. Join using single crochet join on the wrong side to form a strip.

With right side facing, work Sashing Rows 1–7 of Panel One along one long side of strip. Then work Sashing Rows 1–7 of Panel One along other long side of strip.

Panel Four

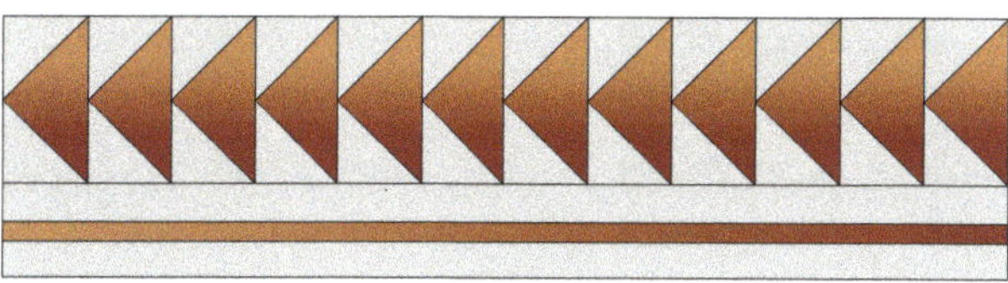

Panel Five

PANEL FOUR

Make four Ohio Star blocks, as shown in Panel Four. Use single crochet join to join the individual squares within the blocks. Join the blocks using single crochet join worked on the wrong side to form a strip.

PANEL FIVE

Make flying geese same as Panel One.

With flying geese pointing to the right, work Sashing Rows 1–7 of Panel One.

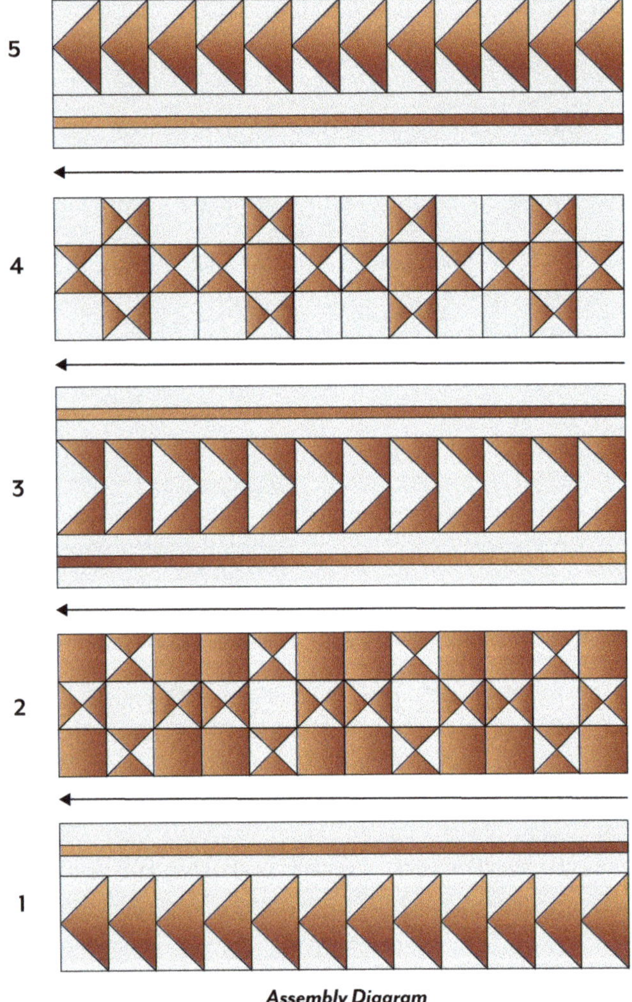

Assembly Diagram

ASSEMBLE

Join the five panels with single crochet on the wrong side, following the Assembly Diagram for placement.

BORDER

Round 1: Using the larger hook, with right side facing, join B in any corner space. 2ch, (1dc, 2ch, 2dc) in same corner space, 1dc in each st around, working (2dc, 2ch, 2dc) in each corner space, sl st in first dc to join.

Round 2: Sl st in corner space, turn. 2ch, (1dc, 2ch, 2dc) in same corner space, 1dc in each st around, working (2dc, 2ch, 2dc) in each corner space, sl st in first dc to join. Fasten off.

RIBBED EDGING

Row 1: With right side facing and using smaller hook, join B in corner at beginning of one short edge, 2ch, 1dc in same st and in each st across. [133dc].

Row 2: 1ch, turn, 1sc in each st across. [133sc].

Row 3: 2ch (counts as first dc), turn, 1 fpdc around the dc 2 rows below that is directly below next st. *1dc in next st of Row 2, 1fpdc around the dc 2 rows below that is directly below next st; repeat from * across.

Rows 4–17: Repeat Rows 2 and 3 seven times. Fasten off.

Work Ribbed Edging on the other short side.

FINISHING

Weave in ends. Steam block to finished size.

LOVE NOTES THROW

The beauty of repeating the same block is highlighted when using an ombre collection of yarns. Here, the subtle variation in tones of the spectacular Purl Soho Nine-Note yarn bundle highlights the pulse of these beating heart blocks!

FINISHED SIZE

43" (110 cm) square

YARNS

DK weight (#3 Light)

Shown in: (A) Purl Soho Knitting Yarn (80% extra fine merino wool, 20% baby alpaca: 219 yd [200 m]/3.5 oz [100 g]). (B) Purl Soho Nine-Note Bundle (80% extra fine merino wool, 20% baby alpaca: 100 yd [91 m]/1.75 oz [50 g].

Note: 1 bundle is 900 yd [823 m] total.

Colors & Quantities

Yarn A – Heirloom White, 6 skeins

Yarn B – Dragon Fruit, 1 bundle

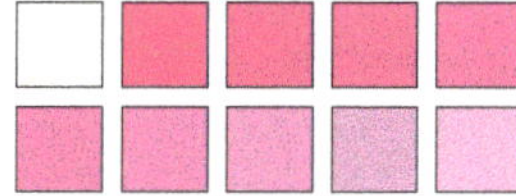

HOOKS

Size G/6 (4 mm)

Size H/8 (5 mm), for Moss stitch border only

NOTIONS

Scissors and yarn needle for weaving in ends.

NOTES

- The Nine-Note Bundle is a carefully calibrated scale of nine skeins ranging from very pale to very saturated. Feel free to substitute other colors, keeping in mind that you need about 100 yd (91 m) in each of nine colors or 900 yd (823 m) total.
- The sample shown uses the JAYG method to join pieces of the block together, but sc join in the back loops only would give a wonderful extra texture to this design.

Special Stitch

U.S. – Double crochet two together (dc2tog) U.K. –Treble crochet two together (tr2tog)

Yarn over, insert hook in next st and pull up a loop (3 loops on hook). Yarn over, pull through 2 loops (2 loops on hook). Yarn over, insert hook in next st, pull up a loop (4 loops on hook). Yarn over, pull through 2 loops (3 loops on hook), yarn over, pull through 3 remaining loops on hook.

LOVE NOTES THROW

INSTRUCTIONS

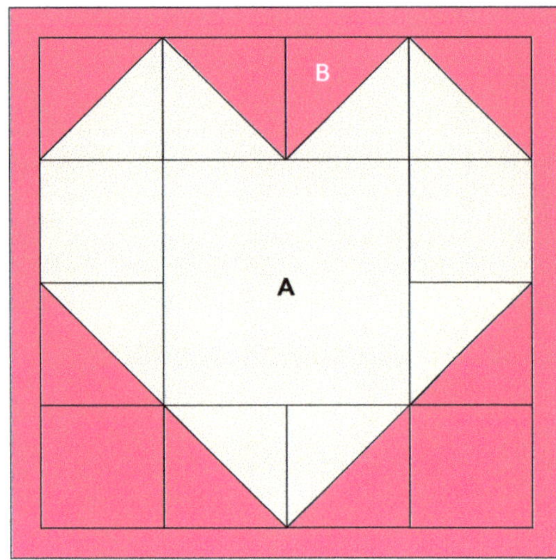

Make nine

MAKE THE BLOCKS

Using A for the heart and B for the outer area, make nine Heart blocks (p. 56).

Note: Since these hearts are all one color, you can substitute a 6-round granny square for the center. Or, if you prefer, you can make four 3-round granny squares for the center instead.

To give the hearts more prominence, omit the optional edging given in the instructions for this block, and work the following:

Edging Round 1: With the wrong side facing, join B in any corner space, 2ch (counts as first dc here and throughout), 2dc in same corner space, *3dc in the next 2 spaces between clusters. 1dc in the right-hand corner space where two squares join, dc2tog, starting in the right-hand corner space and finishing in the left-hand corner space 1dc in the left-hand corner space * Repeat from * to * to next outside corner. (3dc, 2ch, 3dc) in the corner space. Work around in the same manner until you reach the corner you started in, 3dc in last corner space, 2ch, sl st in first dc to join.

Edging Round 2: Sl st into corner space, turn, 2ch, 2dc in same corner space. 3dc in each space around, working (3dc, 2ch, 3dc) in next 3 outside corner spaces until you reach the corner you started in, 3dc in the last corner space, 2ch, sl st in first dc to join. Fasten off.

Edging Round 3: With the right side facing you, join A, 1ch, (1sc, 2ch, 1sc) in same corner space, 1sc in each st around, working (1sc, 2ch, 1sc) in each corner space, sl st in first sc to join. Each side will have 44 sc, including corners.

Edging Round 4: Sl st in corner space, 2ch, (1dc, 2ch, 1dc) in same corner space,1dc in each st around, working (1dc, 2ch, 1dc) in each corner space, sl st in first dc to join. Fasten off. Each side will have 46 dc.

JOIN THE BLOCKS

Using A and single crochet join on the wrong side, join your blocks following the assembly diagram. Note that blocks are arranged using numbers 1–9 to correspond to the nine shades in the Nine-Note bundle with 1 the darkest and 9 the lightest. Make the vertical joins first, followed by the horizontal joins.

When joining your blocks, work through the back loops only of corresponding stitches and through all loops of the corner spaces. This frames the blocks and gives the effect of stitching.

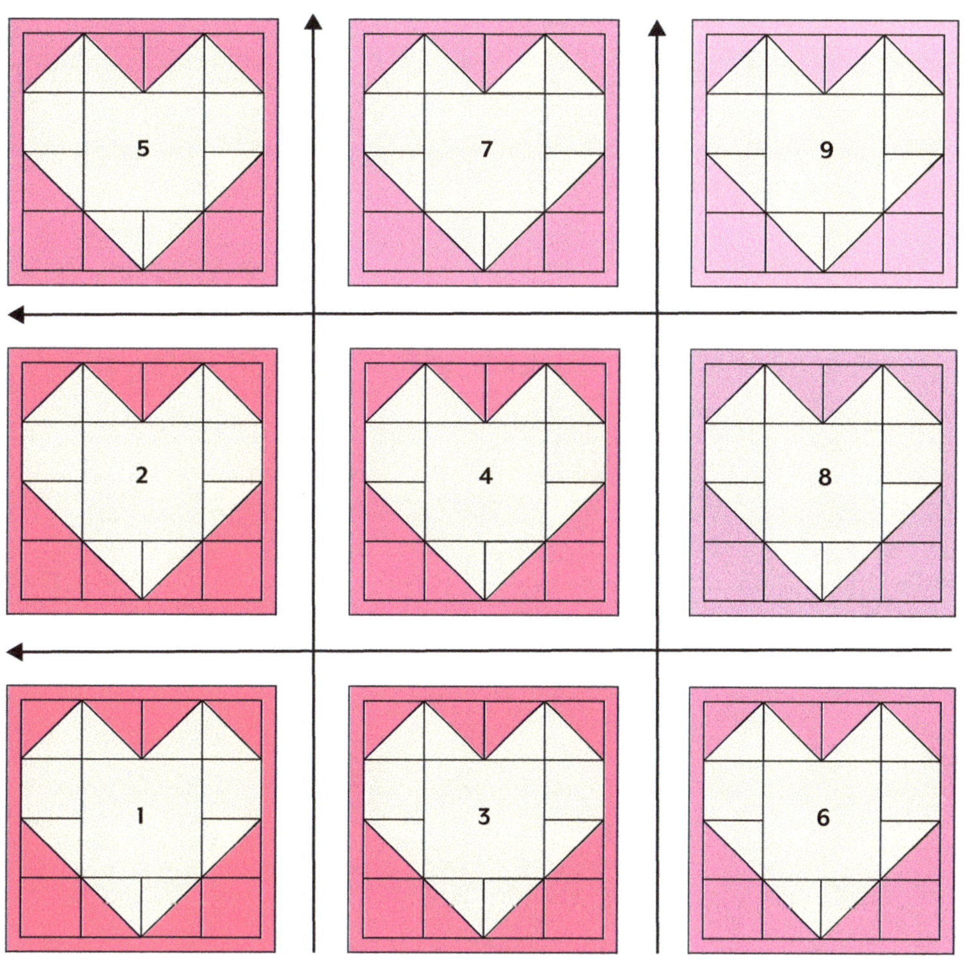

Assembly Diagram

MOSS STITCH BORDER

Round 1: With smaller hook and the right side facing you, join A in any corner space, 1ch, (1dc, 2ch, 1d) in same corner space, 1dc in each st around, working(2dc, 2ch, 2dc) in each corner space, sl st in first dc to join. Fasten off.

Round 2: With the right side facing you, join yarn B (see note) in any corner space, 1ch (2sc, 2ch, 1sc) in same corner space, 1sc in each st around, working (2sc, 2ch, 1sc) in each corner space, sl st in first dc to join. Fasten off.

Note: The (2sc, 2ch, 1sc) in the corner spaces will change the stitch count of each side from an even number of stitches to an odd number of stitches. This is required for Round 3.)

TIP ***Use the Odds and Ends of B for Round 2***
I wanted to use up as much of the Purl Soho yarn as possible. There wasn't enough left to edge the whole blanket in the same shade, so instead, I used the shade corresponding to the block it is edging. I've changed the yarn in the last pull through of the sc that falls in the center point where two blocks join. This stitch is obvious when you are working this round, so you won't need to count stitches. Using the yarn in this way also preserves the ombre effect.

Round 3: With larger hook and the right side facing, join yarn A in any corner space,1ch, (1sc, 2ch, 1sc) in same corner space, *1ch, sk 1 st, 1sc in next st* Repeat from * to * around, working (1sc, 2ch, 1sc) in each corner space, sl st in first sc to join.

Note: Changing to a larger hook will ensure your moss stitch border lays flat.

Rounds 4–14: Sl st into corner space, 1ch, (1sc, 2ch, 1sc) in same corner space, *1ch, sk 1 st, 1sc in next st* Repeat from * to * around, working (1sc, 2ch, 1sc) in each corner space, sl st in first sc to join. Fasten off.

FINISHING

Weave in ends. Steam block to finished size.

MODERN MEDALLION BEDSPREAD

A medallion design, which describes a pattern with a large center block (the "medallion"), is an example of a design that looks extremely complex but is actually simple to make and construct. This is a perfect design to work on over the warmer months, making the smaller individual components. Then, when it cools down, assemble the pieces and enjoy the warmth of your gorgeous new blanket.

FINISHED SIZE

63" (160 cm) square

YARN

DK weight (#3 Light)

Shown in: Stylecraft Life DK (25% wool, 75% acrylic: 326 yd [298 m]/3.5 oz [100g]).

Colors & Quantities

Color A – 2319 Cranberry, 2 balls

Color B – 2344 Fuchsia, 2 balls

Color C – 2417 Lily, 1 ball

Color D – 2301 Rose, 1 ball

Color E – 2305 Cream, 5 balls

Color F – 2445 Parchment, 2 balls

Color G – 2303 Oatmeal, 4 balls

Color H – 2496 Mustard, 1 ball

Color I – 2311 Fern, 1 ball

Color J– 2302 Olive, 1 ball

Color K – 2299 Teal Nepp, 1 ball

Color L – 2298 Duck Egg Nepp, 1 ball

Color M – 2300 White, 1 ball

HOOKS

Size G/6 (4 mm)

NOTIONS

Scissors, yarn needle for weaving in ends, and locking stitch markers (optional).

NOTES

- This blanket is made in sections. First is the center panel, which is then framed by a ring of outer blocks and panels, which give the effect of sashing. I have used single crochet join throughout, but you can use your preferred join or combination of joins.
- You may find it helpful to block each section before joining. It's easier to do with smaller pieces than with a very large, finished blanket like this one.

Special Stitch

U.S. – Double crochet two together (dc2tog)

U.K. –Treble crochet two together (tr2tog)

Yarn over, insert hook in next st and pull up a loop (3 loops on hook). Yarn over, pull through 2 loops (2 loops on hook). Yarn over, insert hook in next st, pull up a loop (4 loops on hook). Yarn over, pull through 2 loops (3 loops on hook), yarn over, pull through 3 remaining loops on hook.

MODERN MEDALLION BEDSPREAD

INSTRUCTIONS

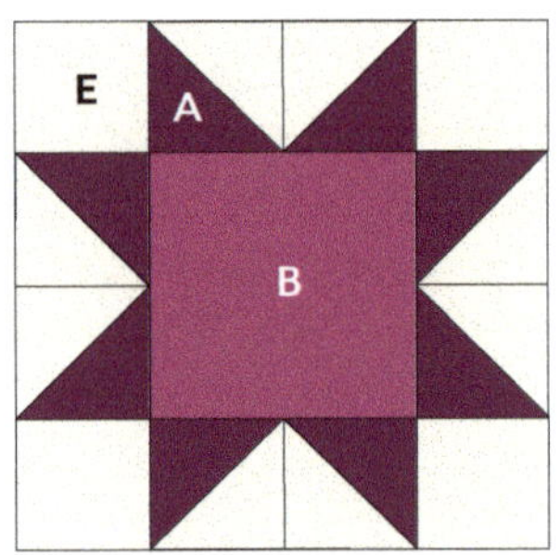

Diagram 1 Make 1

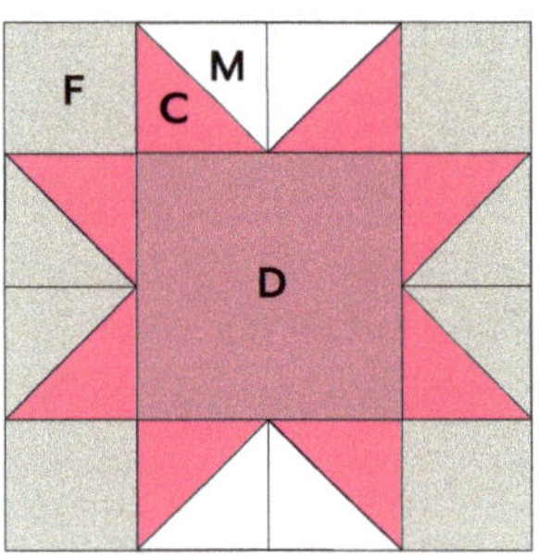

Diagram 2 Make 4

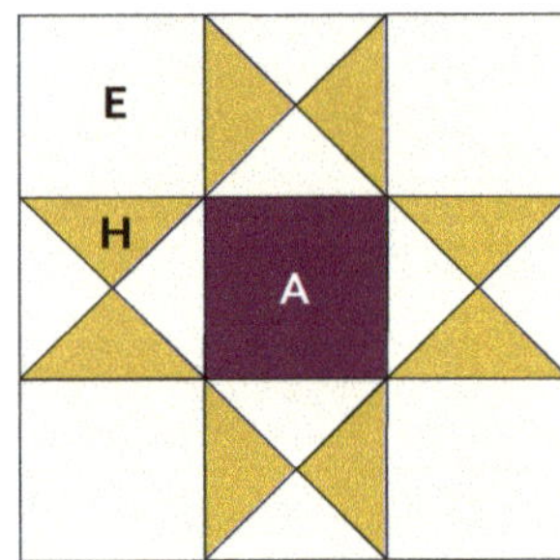

Diagram 3 Make 4

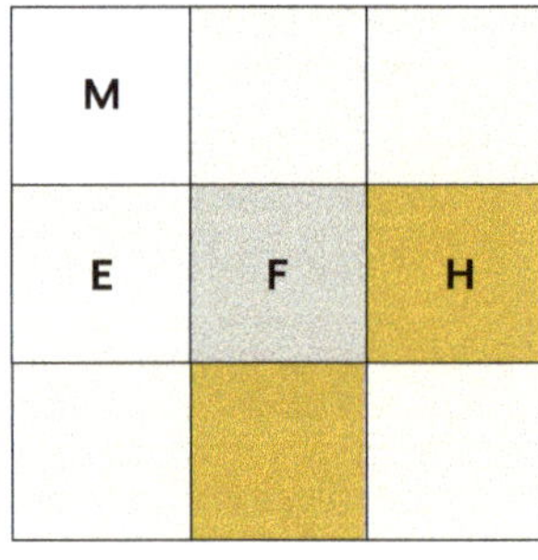

Diagram 4 Make 4

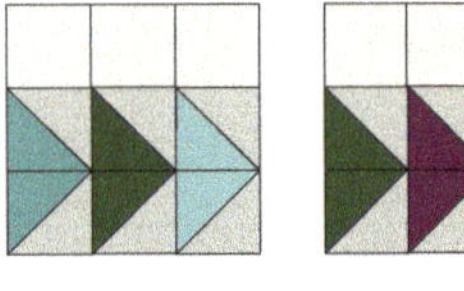

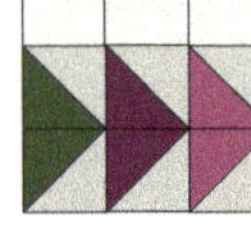

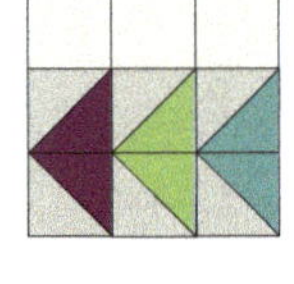

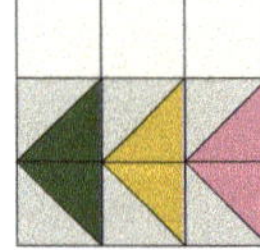

Diagram 5 Flying Geese Units: Make 4 each pointing left and pointing right

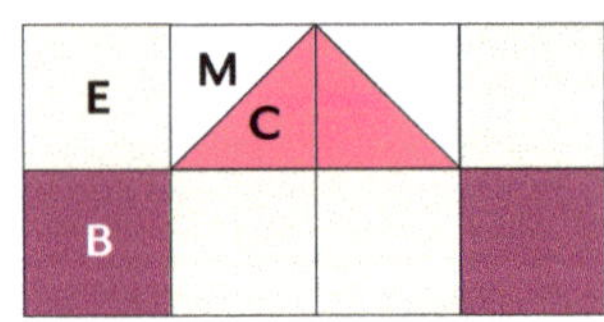

Diagram 6 Mixed Blocks: Make 4

CENTER PANEL

Make Blocks

Omitting the optional edging given in the instructions for these blocks, make the following blocks to combine into the center medallion. Take care to note placement of colors to achieve the final finished effects.

- One Sawtooth Star blocks (p. 58) using colors A, B and E, Diagram 1.
- Four Sawtooth Star blocks using colors C, D, F, and M, Diagram 2.
- Four Ohio Star blocks (p. 60) using colors A, E, and H, Diagram 3.
- Four Nine Patch blocks (p. 42) using colors E, F, H, and M, Diagram 4.

Make Flying Geese and Granny Squares Panels

Using the flying geese unit instructions (p. 22), make 24 flying geese units using a mixed variety of colors. Then, make 24 3-round Granny Squares (p. 22).

Arrange flying geese and granny squares into strips as shown in Diagram 5 and join together. When complete, you should have eight Flying Geese blocks, four of which point in one direction and four which point in the other direction (when the granny squares are at the top of the strips).

Make Mixed Blocks

Along the blocks outlined above, you'll need to make some "mixed" blocks, which are a combination of basic units.

- Make four flying geese, using C for centers and M for outer triangles.
- Make 16 3-round Granny Squares with E.
- Make eight 3-round Granny Squares with with B.

Join an E granny square to both ends of each Flying Geese block.

Join two E granny squares. Repeat this to make four E colored 2-granny square strips. Add one B granny square to both ends of each of the 2-granny square strips, for a total of four B-E-E-B granny square strips.

With the Flying Geese strips pointing toward the outer edge, join one Flying Geese strip to each granny square strip to make a mixed block, for a total of 4 mixed blocks, as shown in Diagram 6.

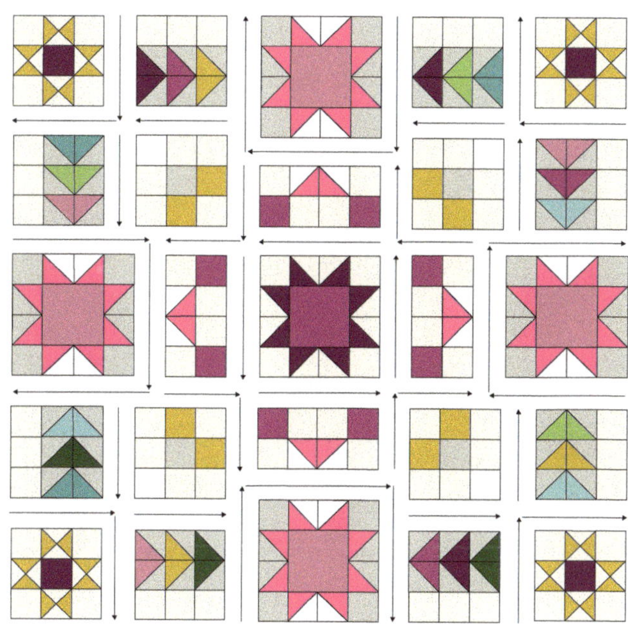

Center Panel Assembly Diagram

JOIN THE CENTER PANEL

Join your center panel blocks together following the Center Panel Assembly Diagram and using single crochet join. Start at the center and work outward.

Note: As long as your blocks are all in the right places, following the joining arrows is not essential. Join your blocks in the way that feels most comfortable for you. It's easy to get lost and end up joining things in the wrong places on large blankets. Try attaching the blocks to each other with stitch markers so you can check they are in the right place before joining.

Once joined, you will have a square panel that measures approximately 41" (103 cm). For a smaller blanket, you could stop here and jump to the border instructions.

Completed Center Panel

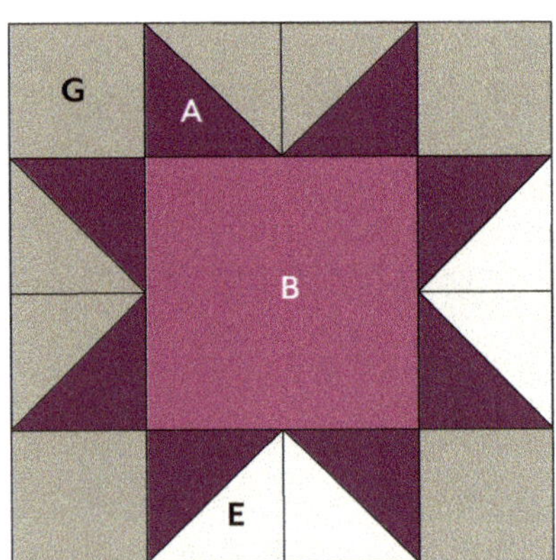

Diagram 7 Sawtooth Star: Make 4

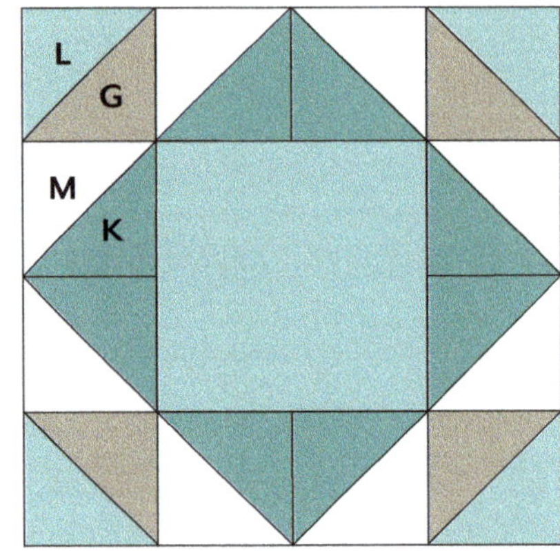

Diagram 8 Mother's Favorite: Make 4

Diagram 9 Flying Geese Panels: Make 8

OUTER RING

Make Blocks

To make the blocks of the outer ring of the quilt, make the following according to their individual block instructions using the colors indicated. Take special care to follow the color placement shown in the diagrams to achieve the unique finished look of this design.

- Four Sawtooth Star blocks using colors A, B, E, and G, and Diagram 7.
- Four Mother's Favorite (p. 46) blocks using colors G, K, L, and M, and Diagram 8.

Make Flying Geese Panels

- Make 48 flying geese using a mix of yarns.

Stack six flying geese units, one on top of the other together so the points travel in the same direction and join them together. Repeat to make a total of eight 6-unit strips.

For each strip, add the sashing as follows:

Row 1: With the wrong side facing you, join yarn G in a corner of the strip so that you are ready to work along a long edge. 2ch (counts as first dc here and throughout), 2dc in same corner space, [3dc in each of next 2 spaces between clusters, 1dc in the right-hand corner space where two squares join, dc2tog, starting in the right-hand corner space and finishing in the left-hand corner space 1dc in the left-hand corner space where blocks join] 5 times. 3dc in each of the next 2 spaces between clusters, 3dc in the next corner space.

Row 2: 2ch, turn, 3dc in each space between clusters across, 1dc in the second ch of starting 2ch.

Row 3: 2ch, turn, 2dc in the first space between first dc and first cluster. 3dc in each space between clusters across ending with 3 dc in space between last cluster and last dc (starting 2ch).

Rows 4 and 5: Repeat Rows 2 and 3.

Row 6: 2 Repeat Row 2. Fasten off.

Turn your strip and repeat Rows 1–6 on the other long edge. You will have a strip of flying geese with a band on sashing top and bottom.

Repeat with the other seven strips of flying geese.

JOIN THE OUTER RING OF BLOCKS

Now it's time to join the outer blocks to your center panel. As with the center panel, it's a good idea to attach your blocks temporarily with stitch markers so that everything is in the right place when you begin to join. Follow the Outer Ring Assembly Diagram provided when joining the blocks as follows:

Join a Mother's Favorite block with a Flying Geese panel on each side to form a strip. Join the strip to the side of the center panel with a single crochet seam. This gives a neat finish and reduces the number of tails you need to weave in.

Repeat on the other three sides of the center panel. Finally, add the four remaining Sawtooth Stars in the corners. Check the orientation of these squares before joining to maintain the cream band around the outside.

BORDER

Round 1: With the wrong side facing, join E in any corner space. 2ch (counts as first dc here and throughout), 2dc in the same corner space, *3dc in the next 2 spaces between clusters, 1dc in the right hand corner space where 2 squares join, dc2tog, starting in the right hand corner space and finishing in the left hand corner space, 1dc in the left hand corner

Outer Ring Assembly Diagram

space.* Repeat from * to * to the next outside corner, (3dc, 2ch, 3dc) in the same corner space. Work around in the same manner until you reach the corner you started in, 3dc in last corner space, 2ch, sl st in first dc to join.

Rounds 2 and 3: Sl st into corner space, turn, 2ch, 2dc in same corner space. 3dc in each space around, working (3dc, 2ch, 3dc) in next 3 outside corner spaces until you reach the corner you started in, 3dc in the last corner space, 2ch, sl st in first dc to join.

Round 4: With the right side facing you, join your chosen yarn in any corner space (I used A). 1ch, (1sc, 2ch, 1sc) in the same corner space, 1sc in each st around, including 1sc in each corner space where squares join, working (1sc, 2ch, 1sc) in each corner space, sl st in first sc to join. Fasten off.

FINISHING

Weave in ends. Steam block to finished size.

Wuthering
Heights

SUPPLEMENTAL MATERIALS

Now that you've been introduced to the world of patchwork granny square blocks, the possibilities are endless! In these next pages, you'll find charts, templates, resources, and other helpful information to help you add your own flair to patchwork crochet projects. I'm looking forward to seeing what you create!

CHARTED INSTRUCTIONS

If you prefer to work from charts, the following charts can be used to stitch granny square, half-square triangle (HST), quarter-square triangle (QST), and flying geese components (pp. 22–29).

Crochet charts are visual representations of crochet patterns, using symbols to depict different stitches, making them a helpful alternative to written instructions. Each symbol corresponds to a specific crochet stitch, and the chart lays out the pattern's structure, showing how the stitches connect and form the overall design.

Crochet chart symbols are universal and the same no matter what language the pattern is written in. Please refer to the key accompanying the charts for symbol definitions.

SYMBOLS KEY	
●	Slip Stitch
⬭	Chain
(double crochet symbol)	Double Crochet
←1	Row number and direction of working

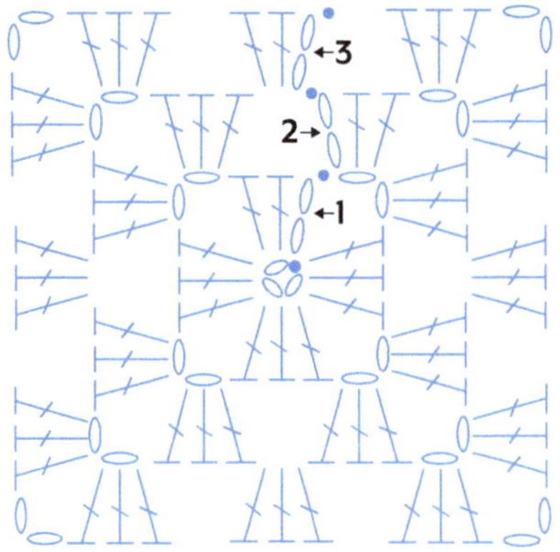

Granny Square

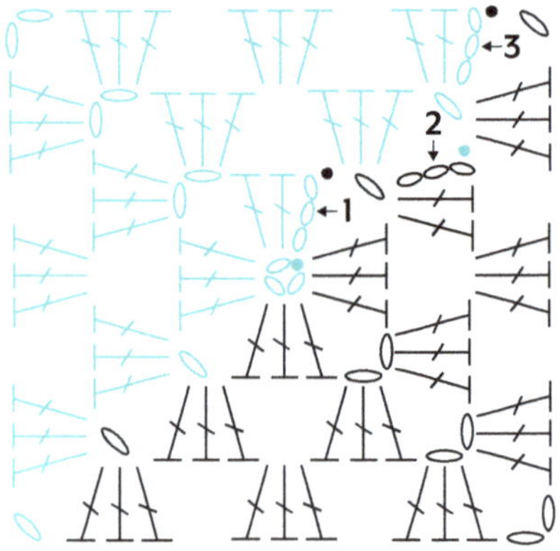

Half-Square Triangle (HST)

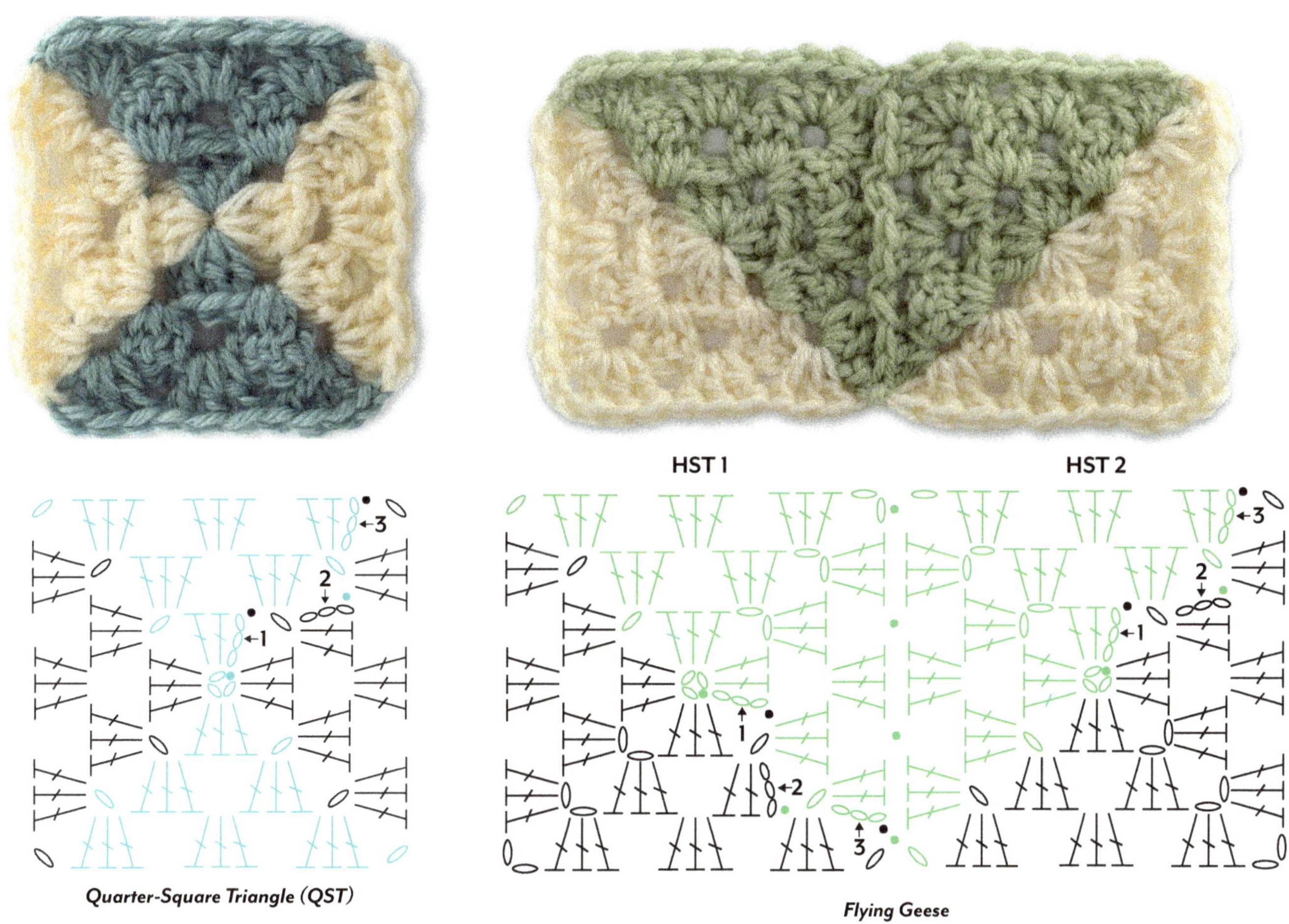

Quarter-Square Triangle (QST)

Flying Geese

CHOOSING COLORS

Choosing colors is deeply personal, and while patterns suggest palettes, they might not always suit your needs. Inspiration is all around us, from the colors in your living room, to a favorite sports team, and especially nature, which offers a stunning array of ready-made color combinations.

COLOR THEORY

To really understand how colors work, let's look at color theory. Color theory is the study of how colors work together and influence our feelings and moods.

The color wheel includes: primary colors (red, yellow, blue) that make all others, secondary colors (orange, green, purple) from mixing two primaries, and tertiary colors (red-orange, blue-green) from primary and secondary mixes. Hues, the pure colors (red, blue, green), are on the outer ring. Tints, lighter pastels, from adding white, are on the inner ring.

Now, you can use some simple rules to create color schemes using the color wheel.

Complementary colors, positioned directly opposite each other on the color wheel, produce a striking visual contrast, making each color appear more vibrant when placed side by side. The Cabin Currents Blanket (p. 87) is an example of a complementary color scheme. Complementary shades of blue and orange sit directly opposite each other on the color wheel.

Analogous colors, those positioned adjacent to each other on the color wheel, create visually harmonious and related color groups. I have used tones of blue, purple, and pink in the Lavender Path Baby Blanket (p. 69). If you are unsure about which colors to pick, analogous color schemes are always a safe choice.

Triadic color schemes employ three colors equally spaced on the color wheel, resulting in a vibrant yet balanced visual effect. The even spacing ensures harmony, while the color contrast creates a lively feel. I have used a triadic color scheme, underpinned by bright red, blue, and yellow in the Kaleidoscope Cushion Set (p. 81).

Monochromatic color palettes, which rely on variations of a single hue by adjusting its lightness and darkness, create a sense of visual unity. These schemes are pleasing to the eye and effectively direct attention to the subject by limiting the color palette. An example of a monochromatic colour scheme would be the Love Notes Throw (p.117). Varying tints of the same pink draw focus to the hearts.

Complementary colors

Analogous colors

Triadic color schemes

Monochromatic color palettes

DESIGNING YOUR OWN BLANKETS

BLOCK TEMPLATES: CHOOSE YOUR OWN COLORS

The techniques in this book will allow you to recreate a limitless number of quilt blocks in crochet. Here are the basic block designs to allow you to experiment with your own designs. Trace or photocopy them and color them in to try different colorways and experiment with layouts. Remember, some blocks are slightly smaller than others when crocheted and have optional border rows to square them up. Refer to the specific block instructions for details.

Nine Patch

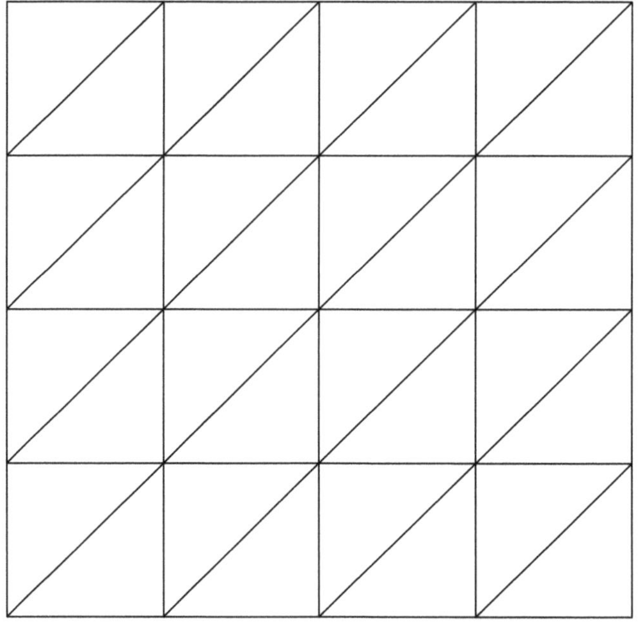

Sails

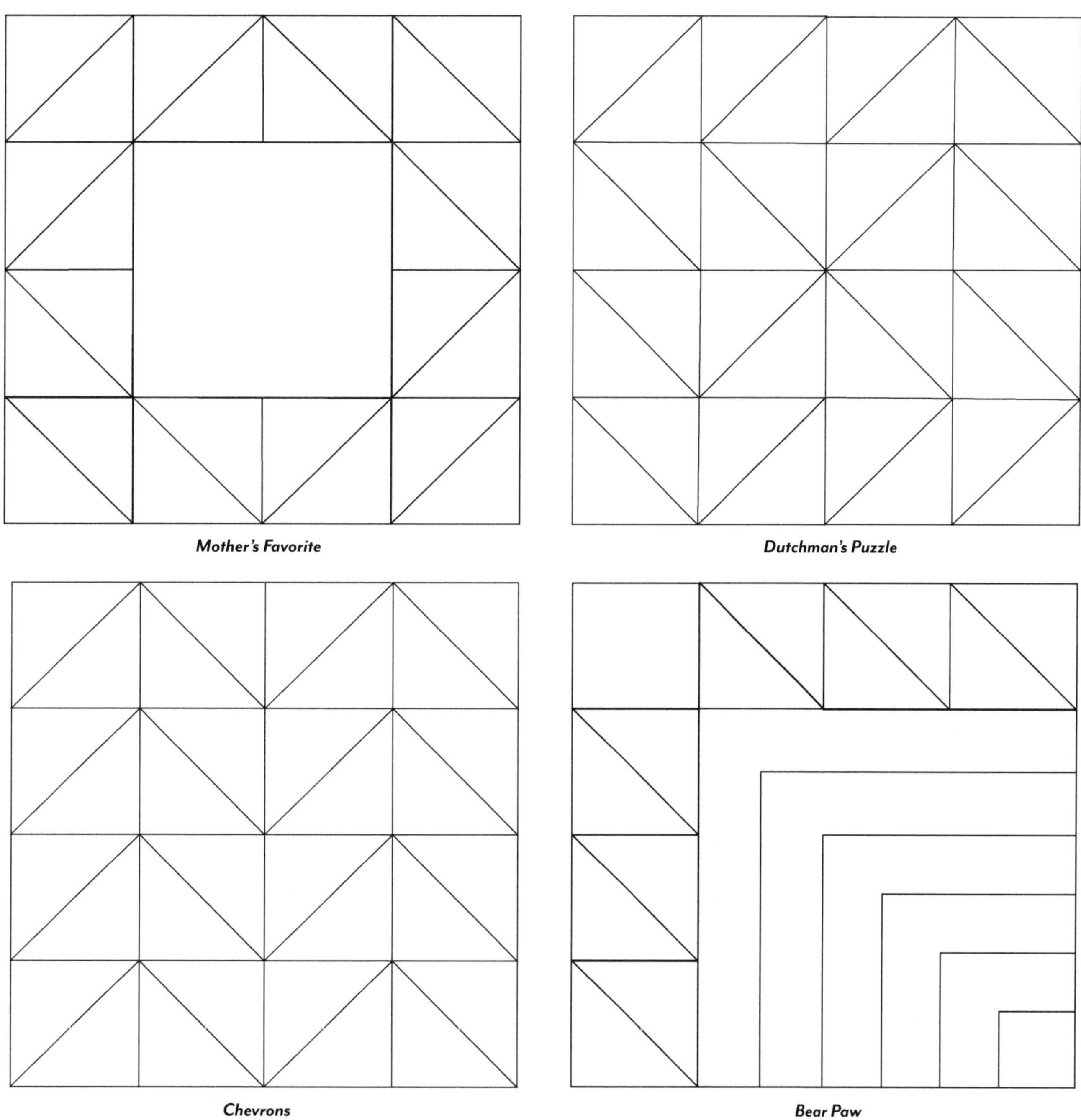

Mother's Favorite

Dutchman's Puzzle

Chevrons

Bear Paw

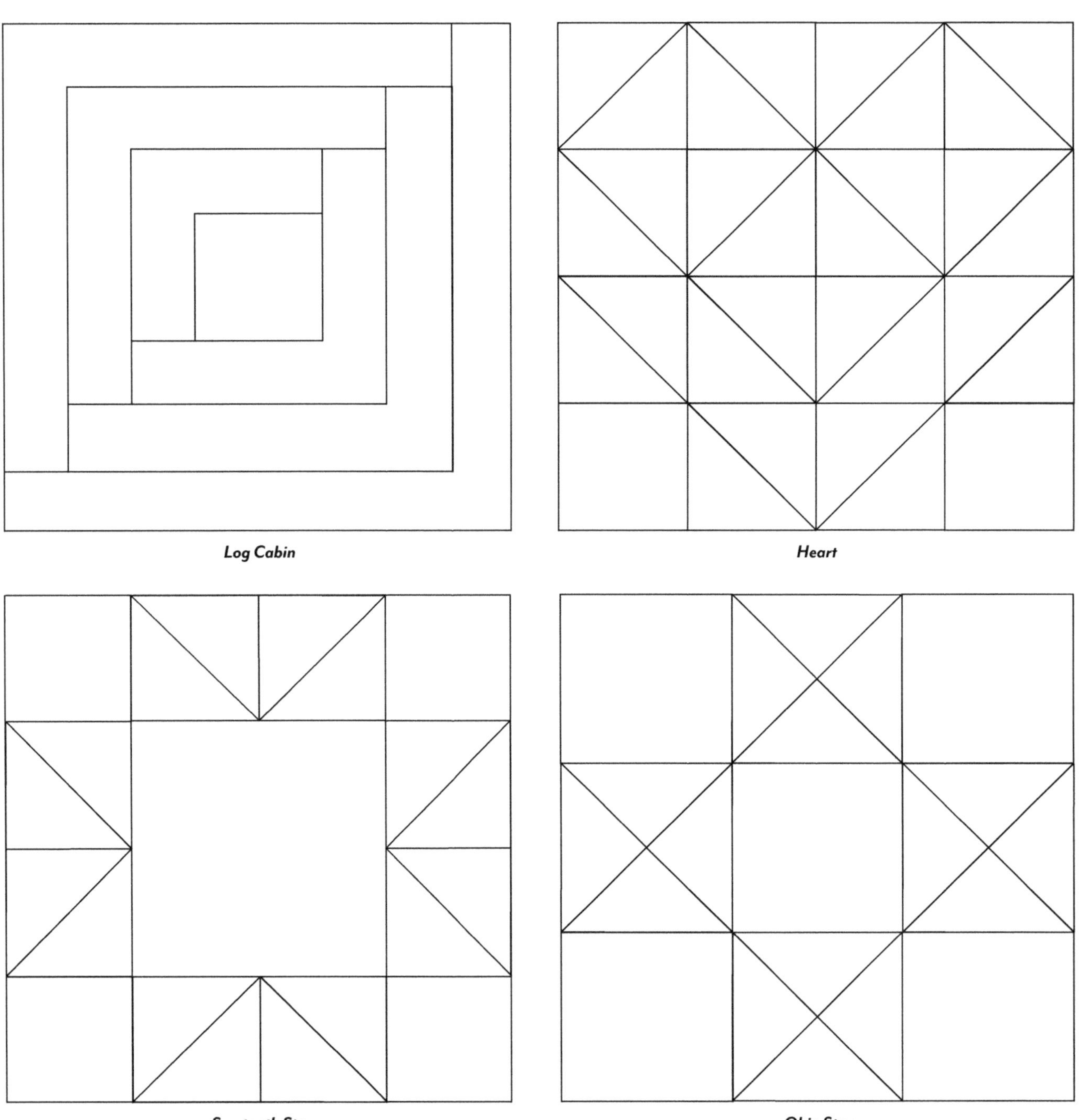

Log Cabin

Heart

Sawtooth Star

Ohio Star

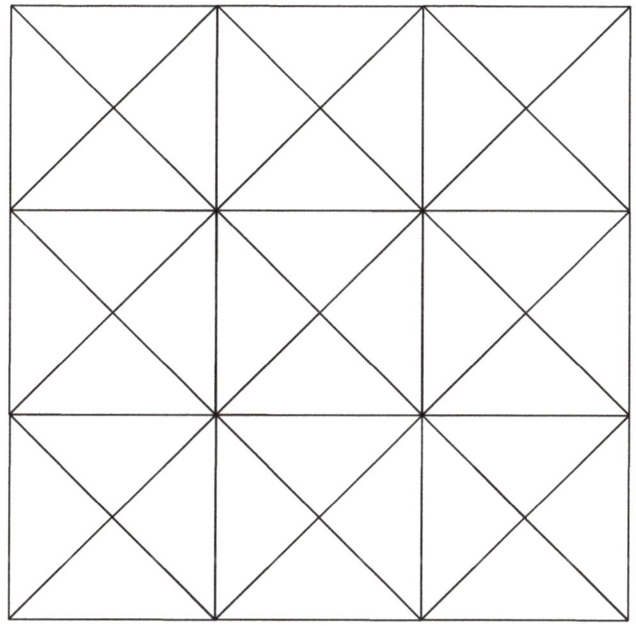

Broken Dishes

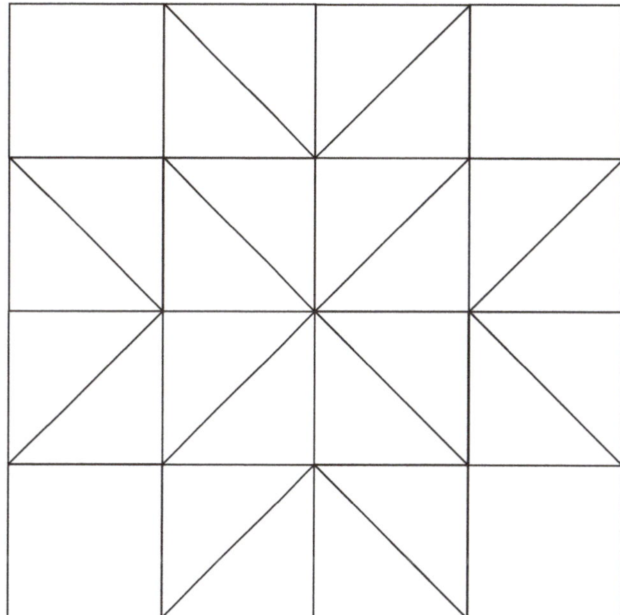

Double Trailing Star

Scan the QR code with your smartphone or visit www.quarto.com/files/PatchworkGrannySquareBlankets to download a printable PDF of these layout templates.

DESIGN YOUR OWN BLANKET LAYOUTS

After you've played with designing your own colorways or your own blocks, take the next step to create your own blanket patterns.

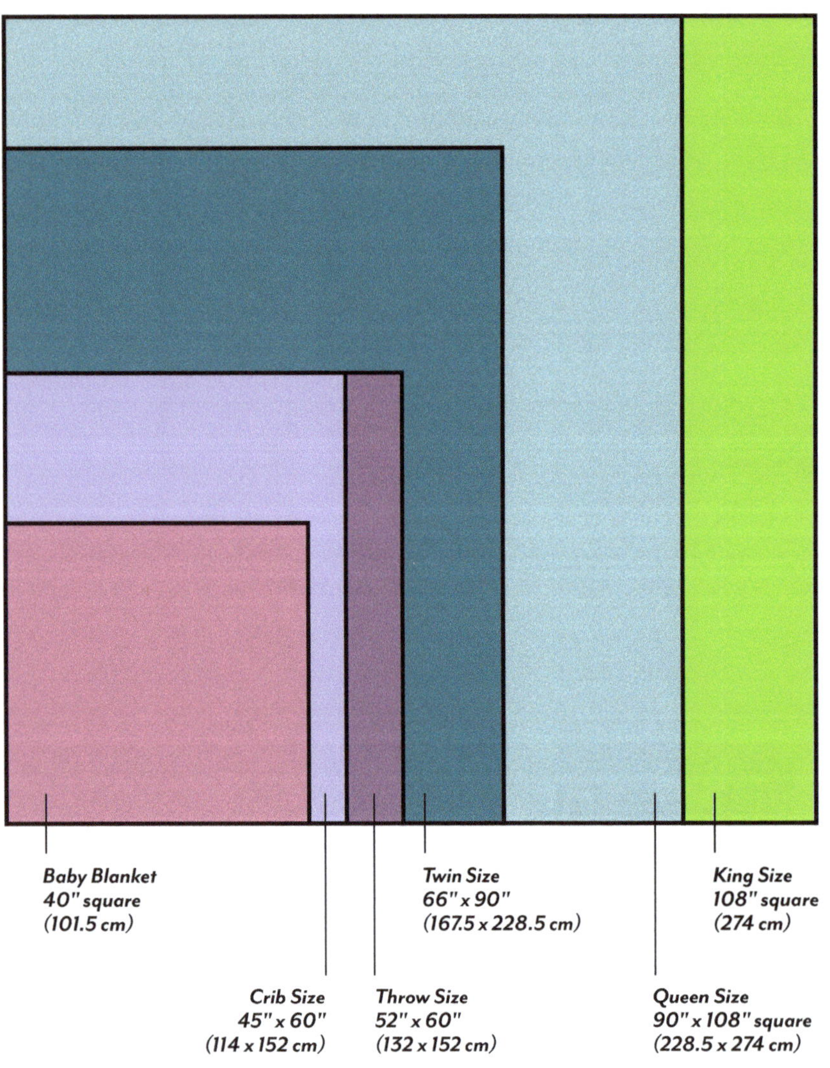

Common Blanket Sizes

Here are some of the most common blanket sizes. Use the size guide in each block pattern to work out how many blocks you will need to make a blanket in the size you want. Remember, the thicker the yarn you are using, the larger the block, so the fewer you will need.

CALCULATING YARN QUANTITIES

When designing your own blankets, you may be wondering how to figure out how much yarn you'll need. A simple way to estimate yarn quantity for granny square patchwork blocks is to start by making a three-round granny square using the yarn and hook you wish to use and then weigh it. You can use this weight to make further calculations.

For example, if your 3-round granny square weighs 2 grams, divide that in half and you have the amount you need for each color in a half-square triangle (1 gram of each color). Divide the weight by four, and you have how much you need for each section of a quarter-square triangle (QST)(.5 gram). You can then multiply this by the number of units you need to make.

Using the Ohio Star as an example and assuming a three-round granny square weighs 2 grams, you would need the following quantities of yarn to make this block.

- Four 3-round Granny Square in white: 2 grams x 4 units = 8 grams
- One 3-round Granny Square in light pink: 2 grams
- Eight QST sections in dark pink: 0.5 gram x 8 units = 4 grams
- Eight QST sections in white: 0.5 gram x 8 units = 4 grams

Once totaled, to make this block, you need 12 grams of white, 4 grams of dark pink and 2 grams of light pink.

For the final step, multiply the amount of yarn needed for an individual block by the number of blocks in the design. Here, if we make a grid of nine Ohio Star blocks, we multiply 12 grams of x 9 blocks, which equals 108 grams of white yarn. Repeat this for each color.

To be on the safe side, most tech editors suggest adding 10% to the total yardage (meterage) required to account for any inconsistency in length in the skein, for swatching, and weaving in ends.

RESOURCES

I'd like to extend a special thanks to the following yarn companies for providing the beautiful yarns featured in this book. Visit their websites or your local yarn stores to purchase the colors and yardage you need to make your projects a reality!

DROPS

garnstudio.com

Drops Yarn is a Norwegian brand offering a wide range of yarns, including fibers like wool, alpaca, cotton, and silk, at affordable prices.

KING COLE YARNS

kingcole.com

This family-run business has been producing yarns for handknitting and crochet in England for nearly 100 years.

KNIT PICKS/WECROCHET

knitpicks.com or crochet.com

Since 2002, Knit Picks has been a beloved online retailer for affordable, colorful yarns. In 2019, Knit Picks' parent company launched WeCrochet, the sister brand specifically for crocheters.

PURL SOHO

purlsoho.com

The team at Purl Soho is dedicated to their customers, providing luxurious fibers to modern makers.

SIRDAR

sirdar.com

Sirdar's origins trace back to 1880, and they have a rich history of producing quality yarns and knitting and crochet patterns.

STYLECRAFT YARNS

stylecraft-yarns.co.uk

Launched in 1989 and providing yarns that makers have loved ever since, Stylecraft Yarns are available from more than 1,000 U.K. retailers and distributed widely around the world.

THE GREY SHEEP CO.

thegreysheep.co.uk

Founded in 2004, this U.K.-based family farm produces beautiful small batch yarns with wool from their own flock.

ACKNOWLEDGMENTS

I still can't quite believe I've had the opportunity to write a book! I am profoundly grateful to my editor, Kerry Bogert, for recognizing the potential in my work and for guiding me so patiently every step of the way.

My deepest thanks to the entire team at Quarto Publishing for their invaluable help and support: art director Kelly Desabrais, designer Samantha J. Bednarek, copy editor Lorraine Savage, tech editor KJ Hay, and editorial director Joy Aquilino.

Thank you to stylist Claire Montgomerie and photographer Leanne Dixon for capturing the beautiful images in this book. Working with you was an absolute pleasure, and I sincerely hope we have the chance to work together again!

Special thanks to Sean Sturdy, who made the Polaris Blanket for me and has provided unwavering support throughout this project.

To Laurelin and Robin, my incredible life support system. You are always there for me, lifting me up whenever doubt creeps in.

I truly appreciate the support from the yarn manufacturers who contributed the wonderful yarns I have used to make the projects.

And of course, to my wonderful family for believing Mum can do anything!

ABOUT THE AUTHOR

Anita Gibney is a lifelong maker of things and is equally happy with a hook or a circular saw.

After crafting with many media, for the last fifteen years she has focused her obsession with color and design on yarn.

She now creates fun and accessible crochet patterns and videos full time and uses her expertise as a teacher to share her love of the craft with others. Anita was the designer of the highly popular Coronation Crochet Along with Sirdar and is also an ambassador for Stylecraft Yarns.

When not working on a new crochet design, Anita will usually be found knitting! Find her designs at madebyanita.com.

INDEX

www.ingramcontent.com/pod-product-compliance
Lightning Source LLC
LaVergne TN
LVHW070022110126
829203LV00007B/9
9780760396254